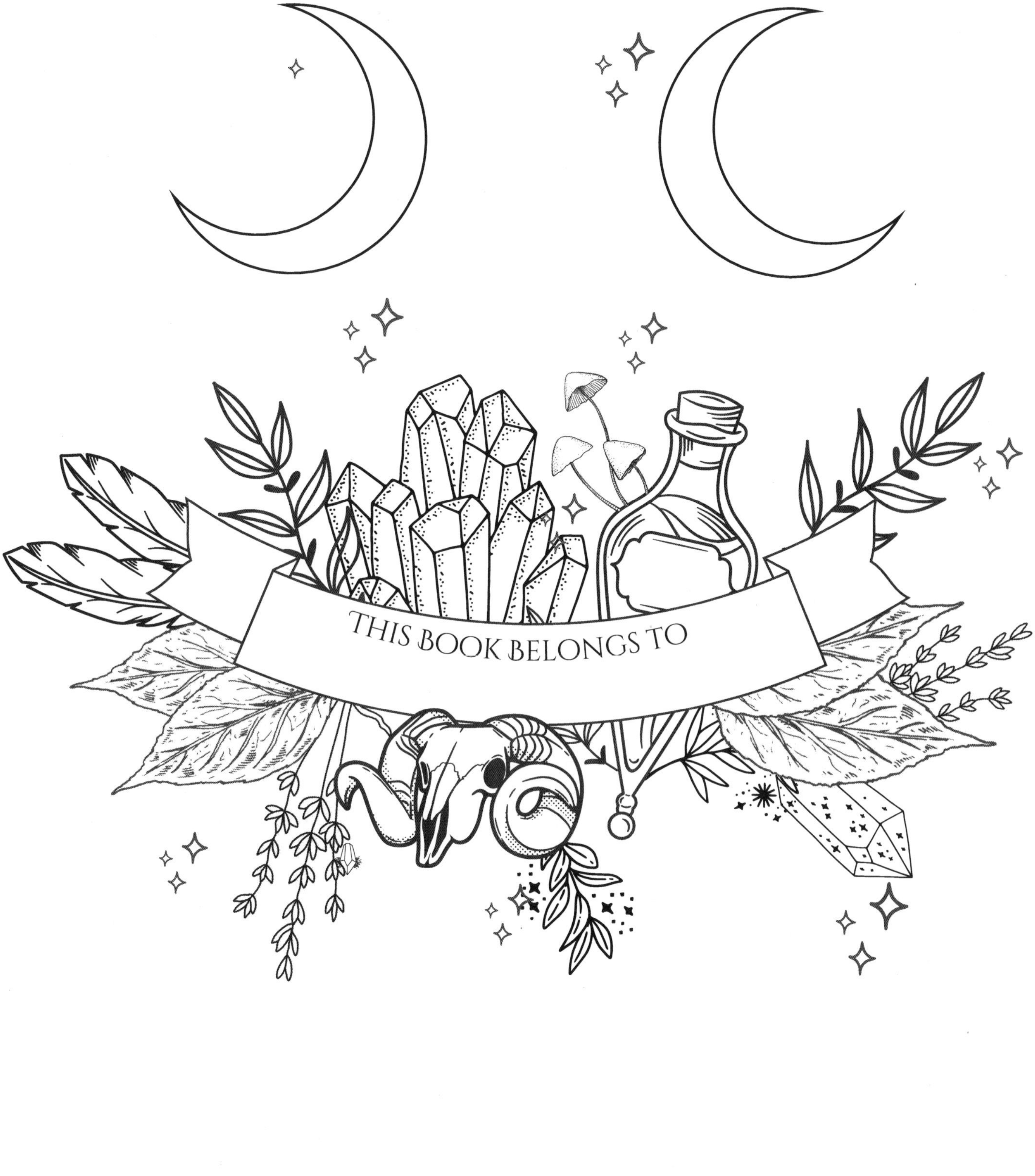
THIS BOOK BELONGS TO

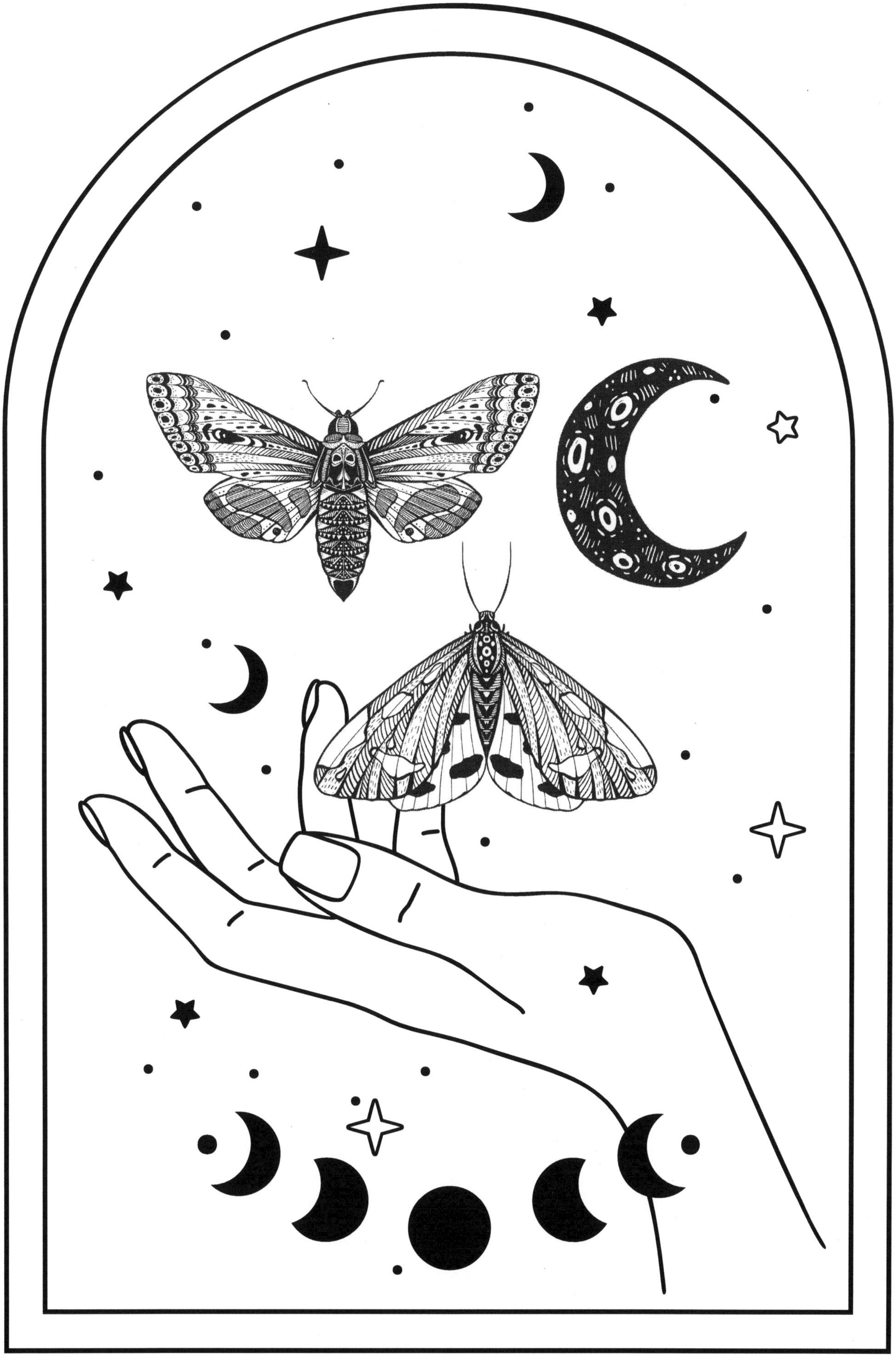

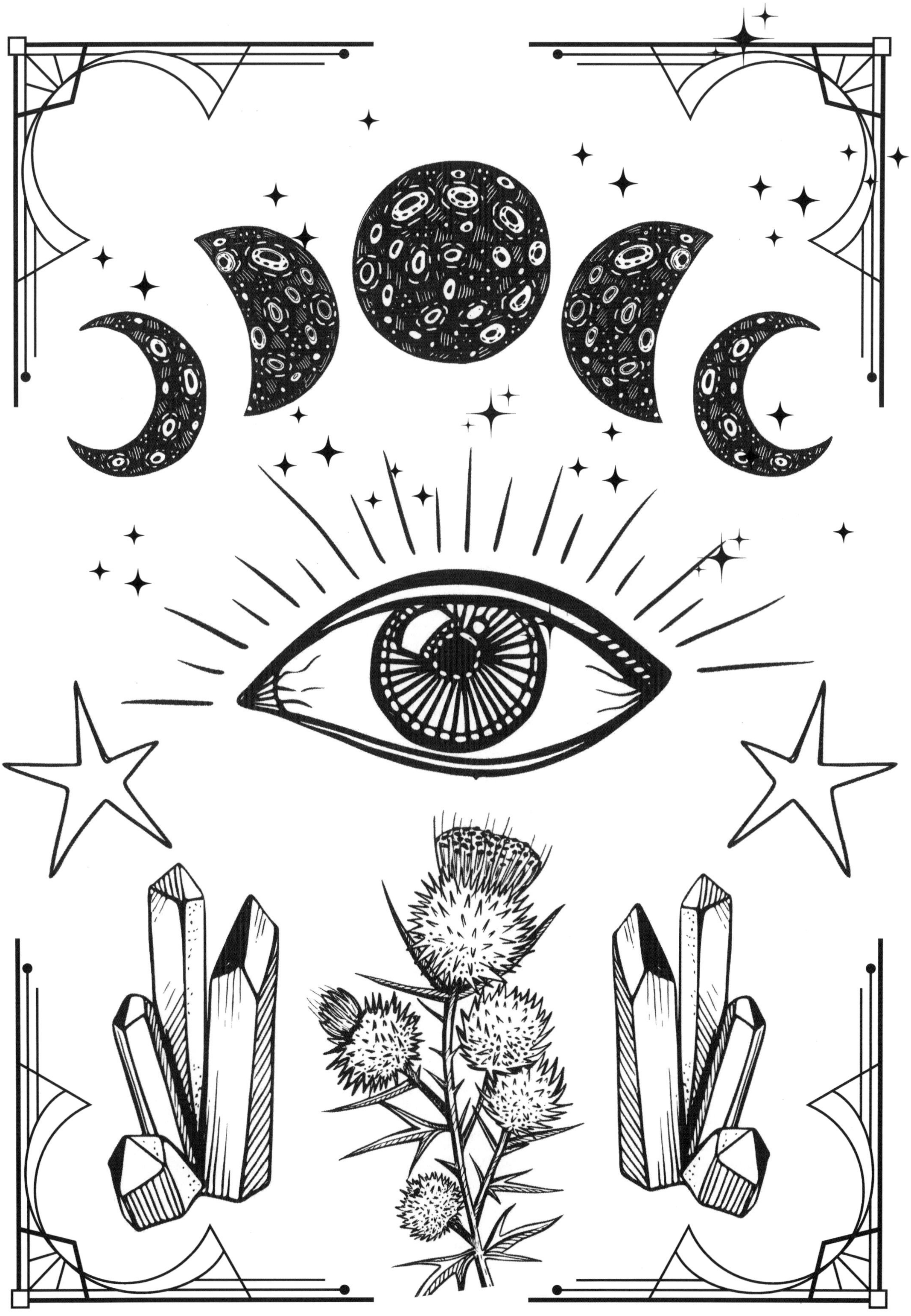

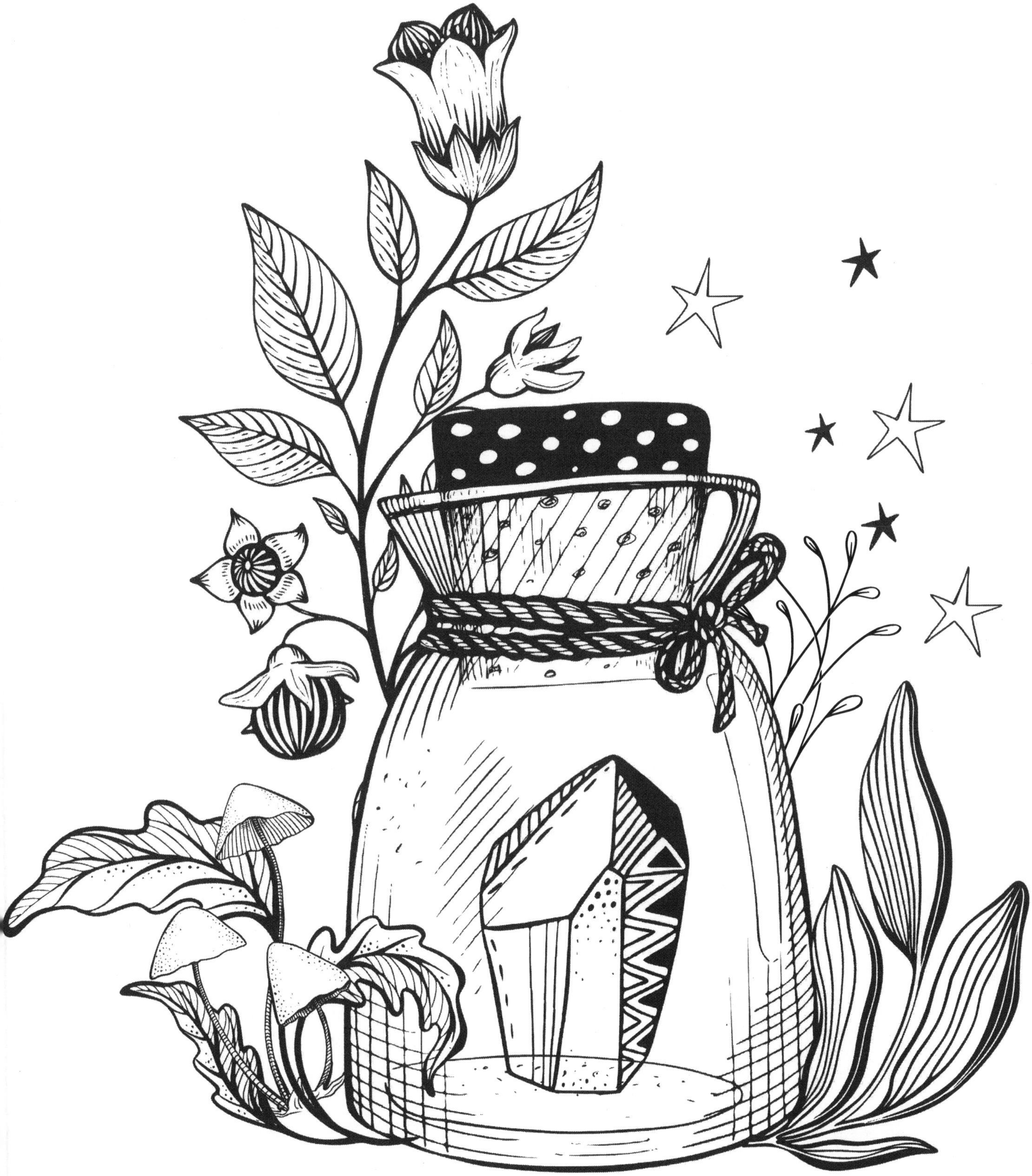

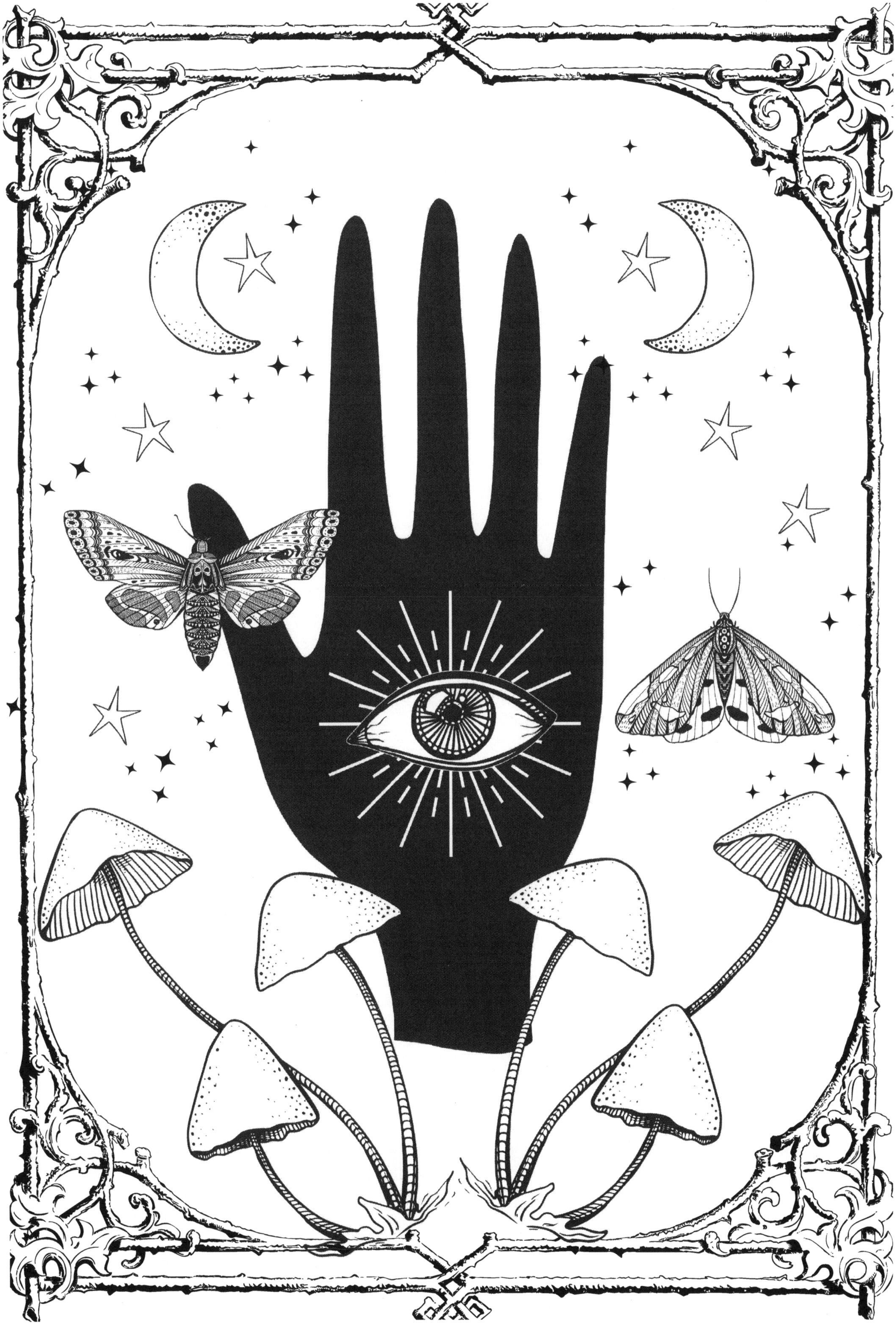

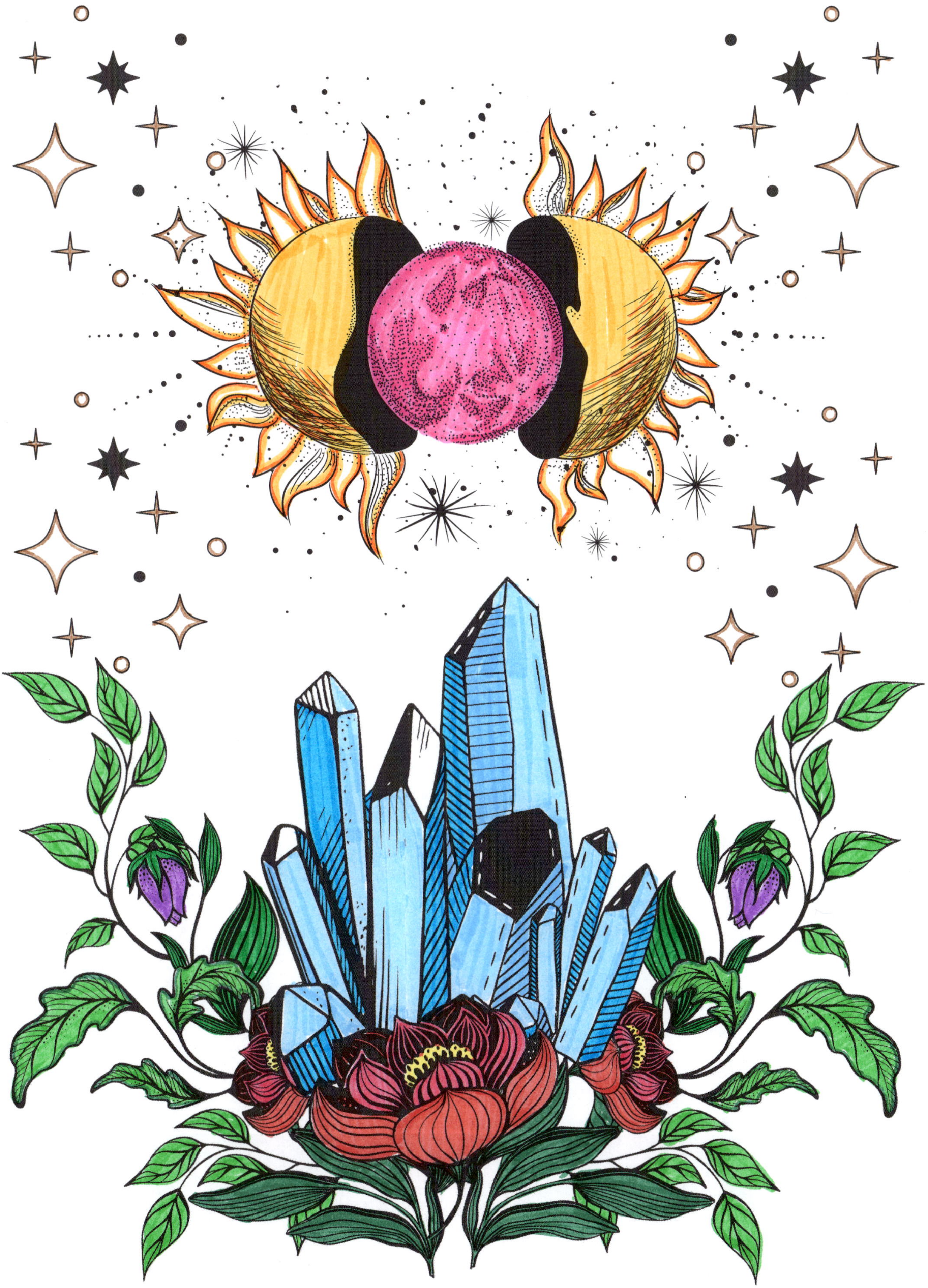

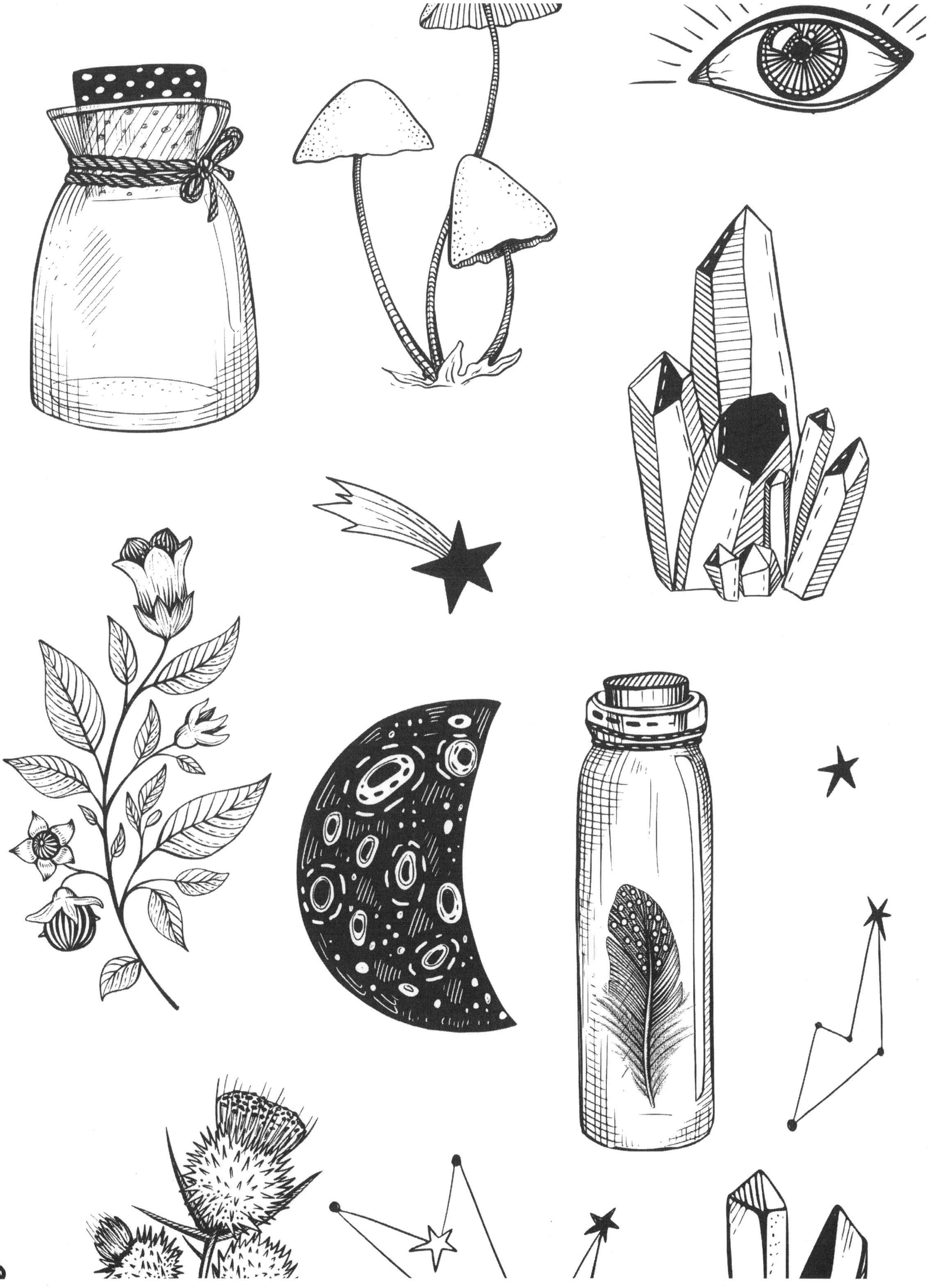

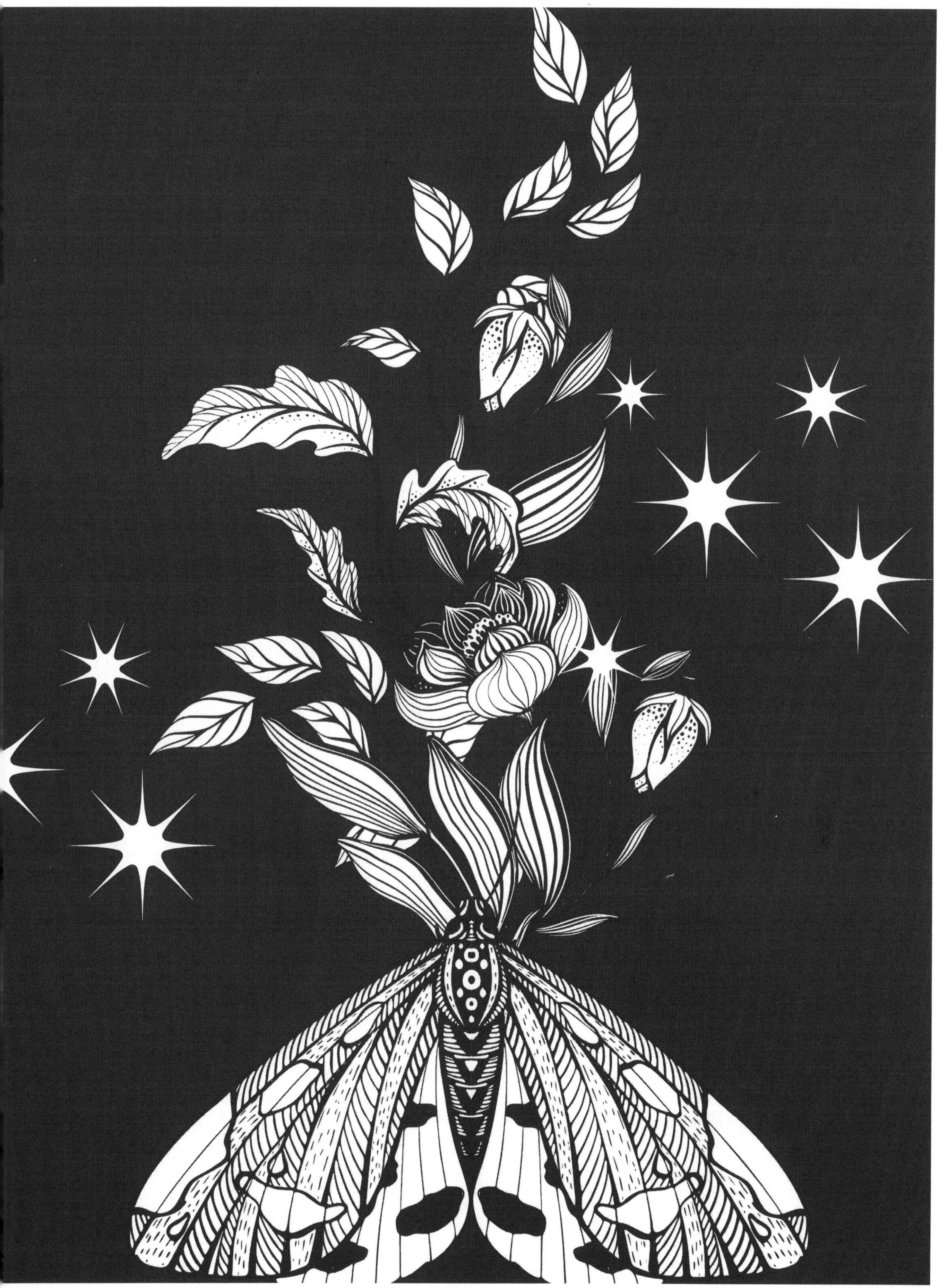

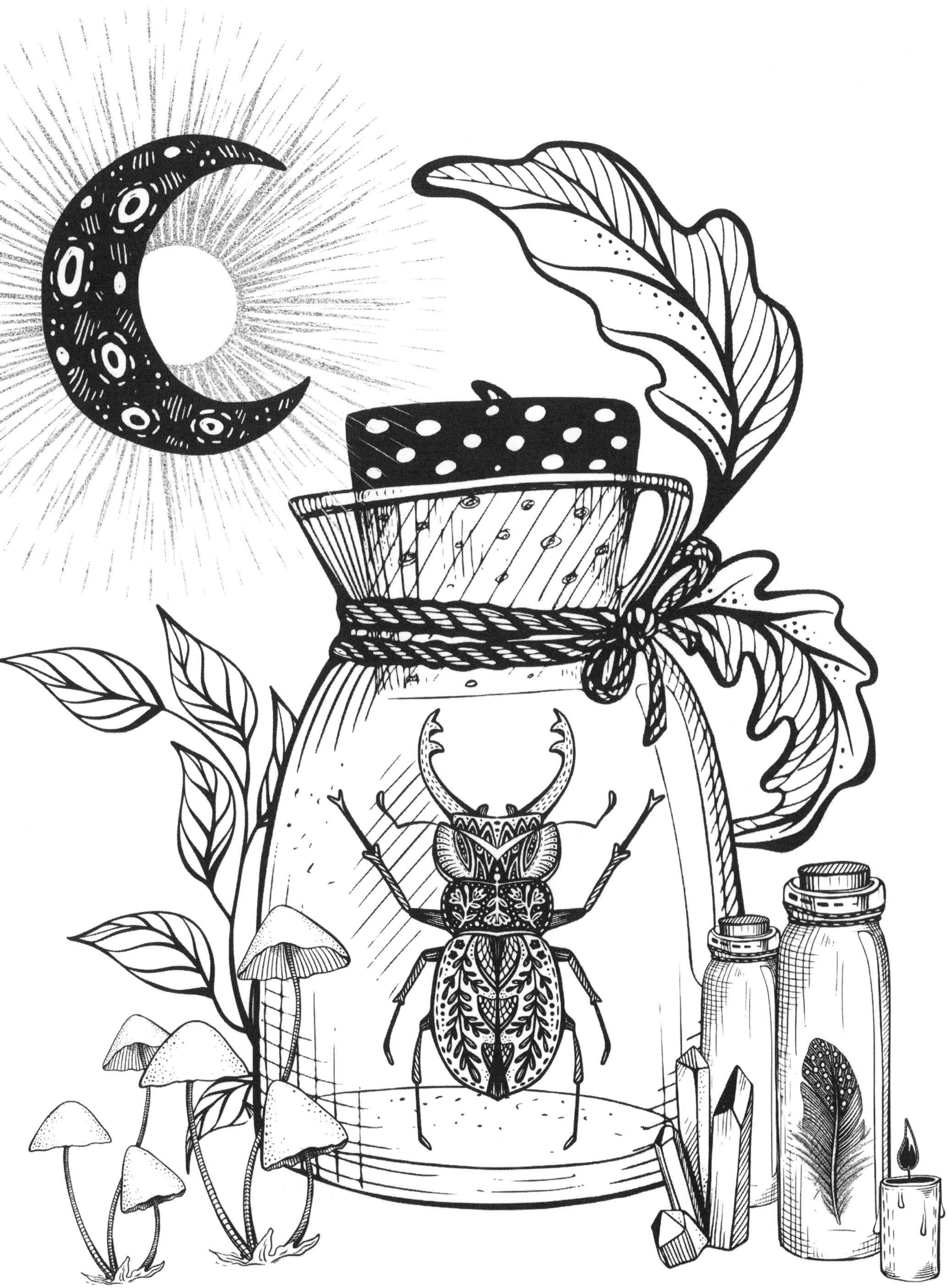

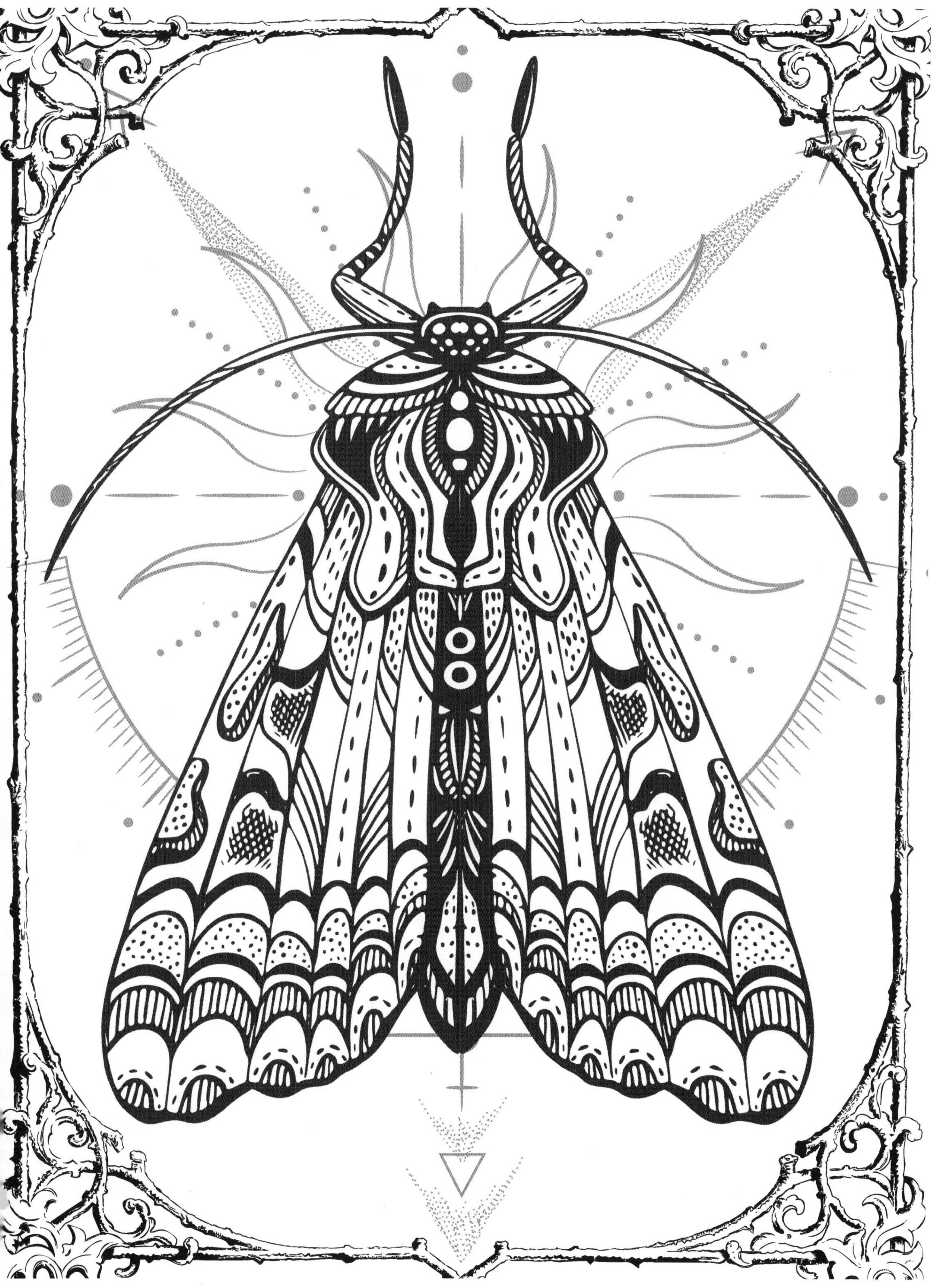

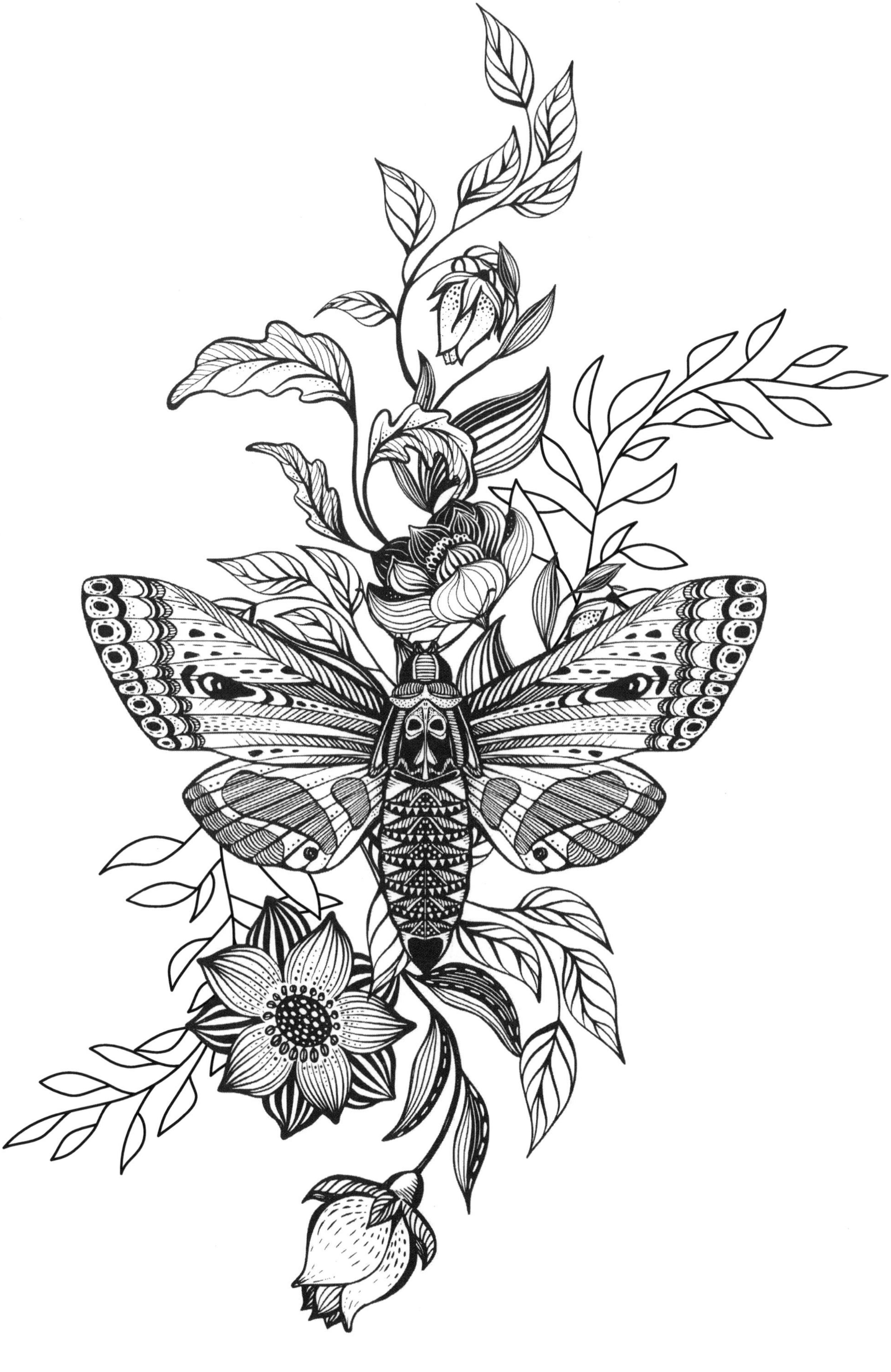

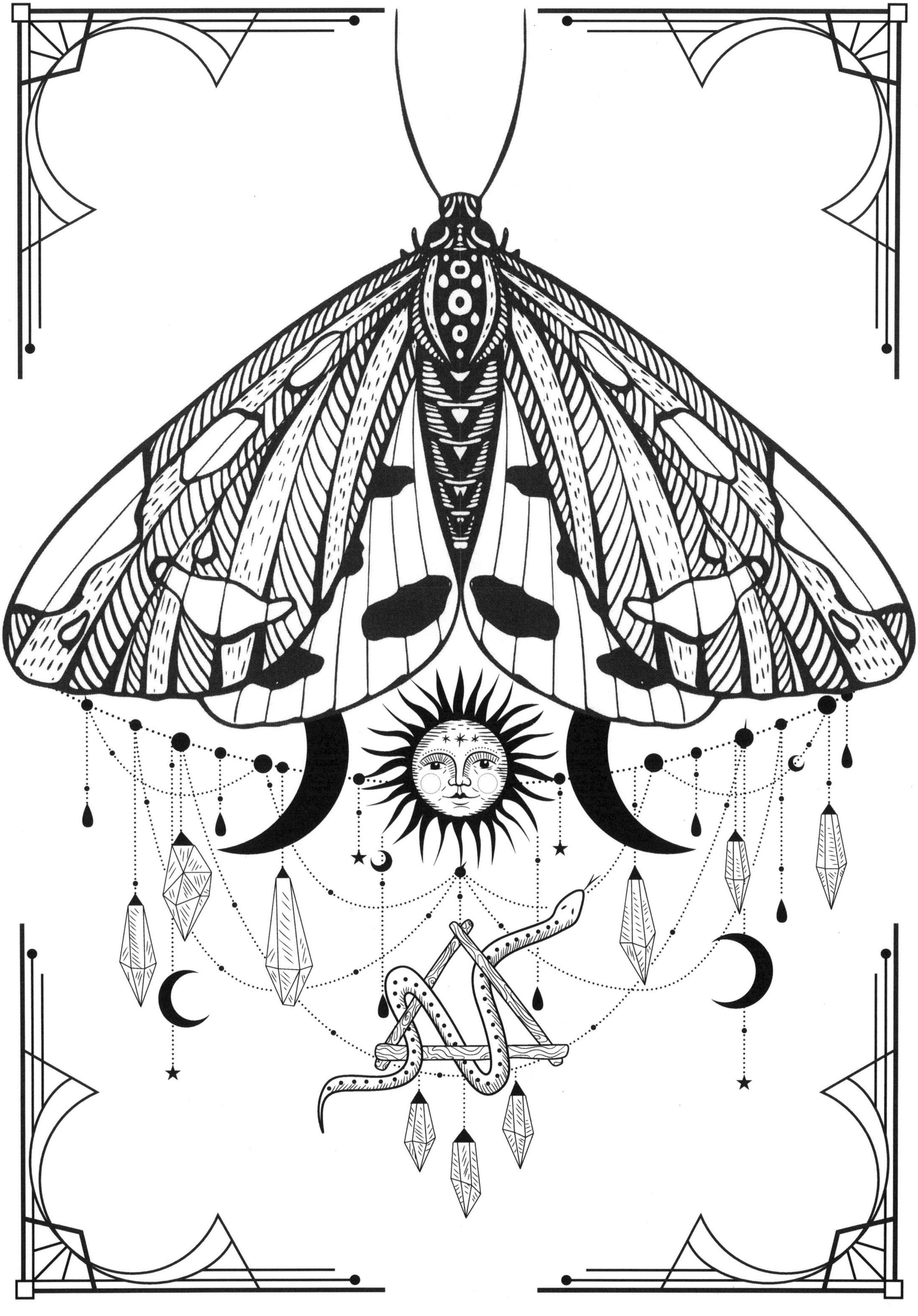

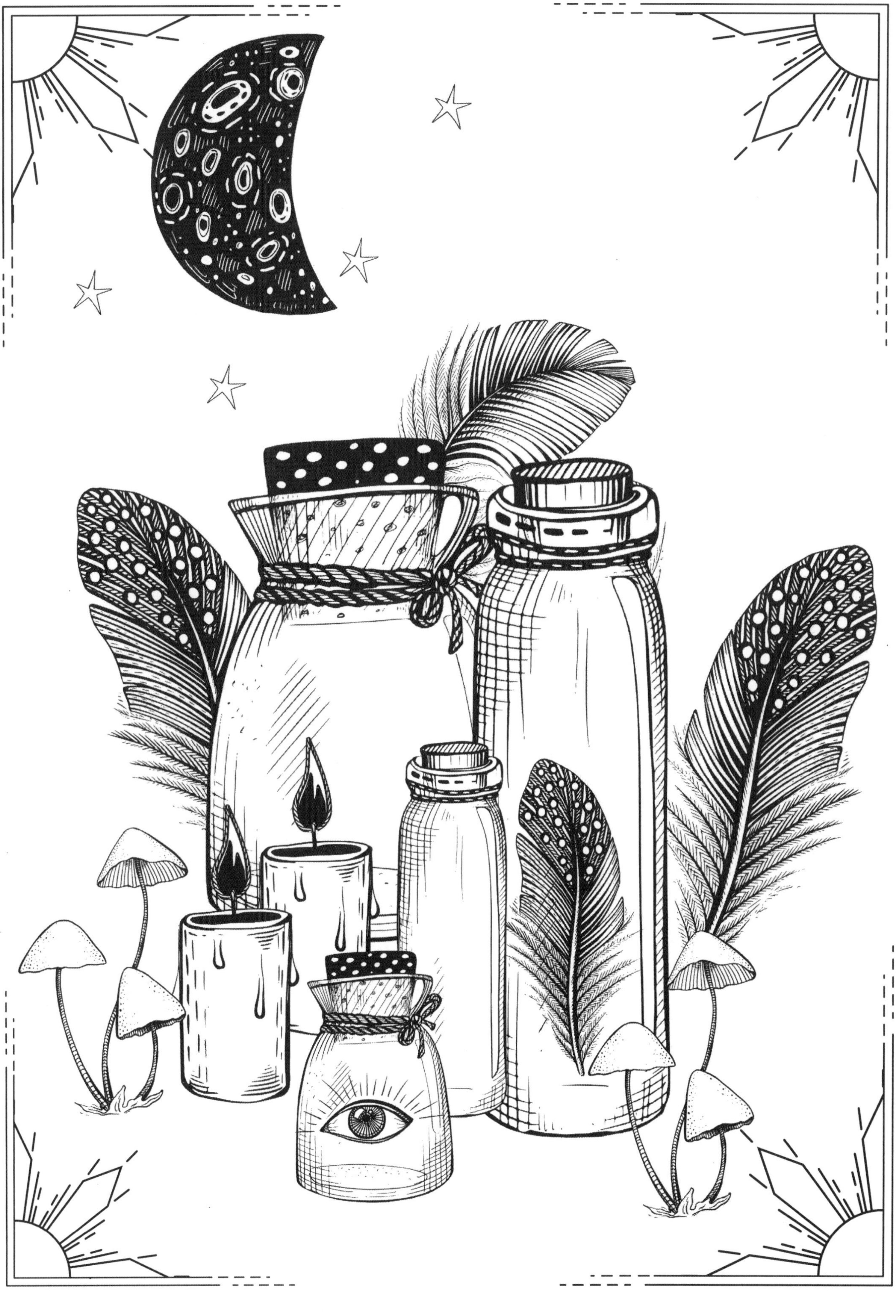

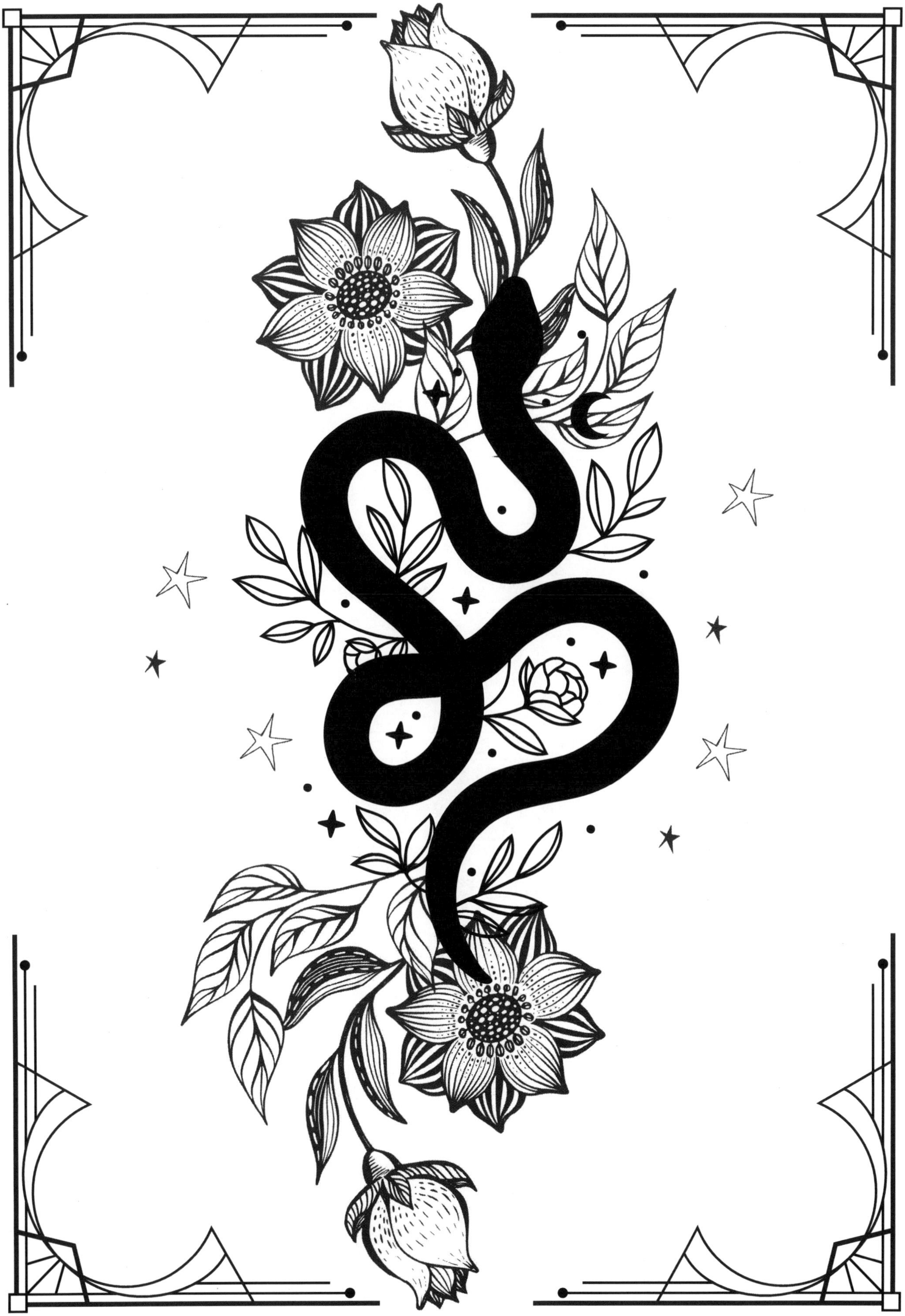

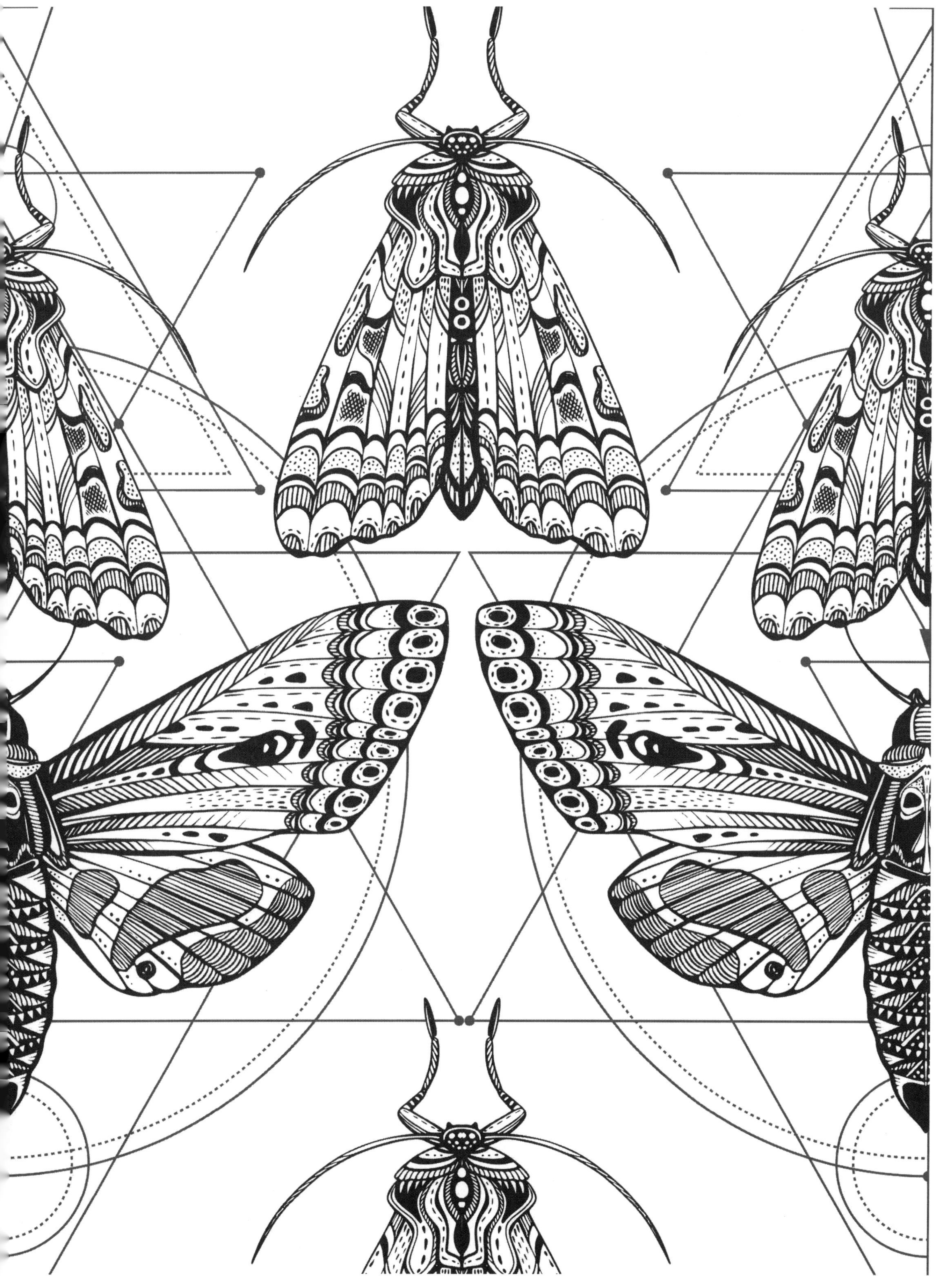

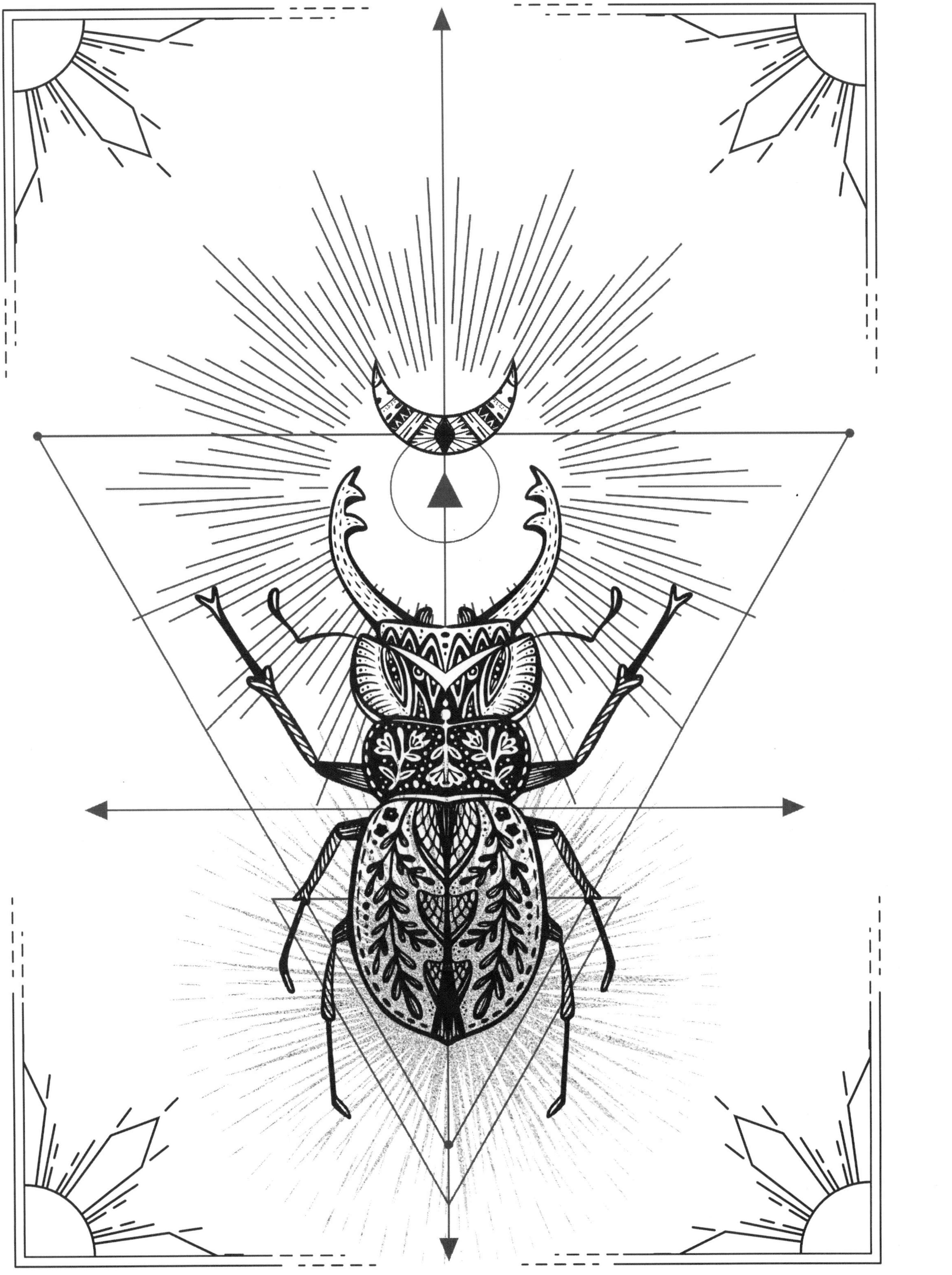

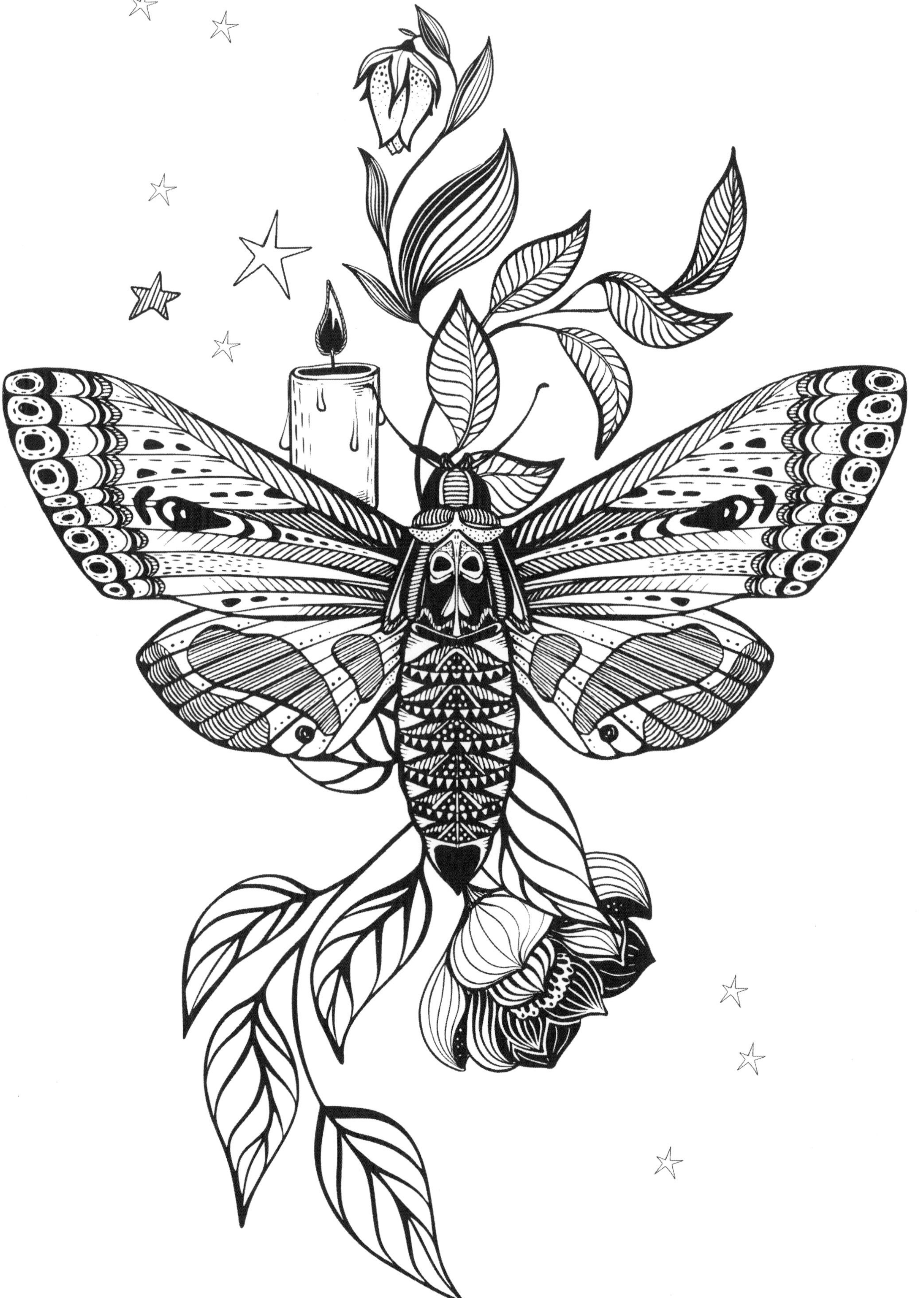

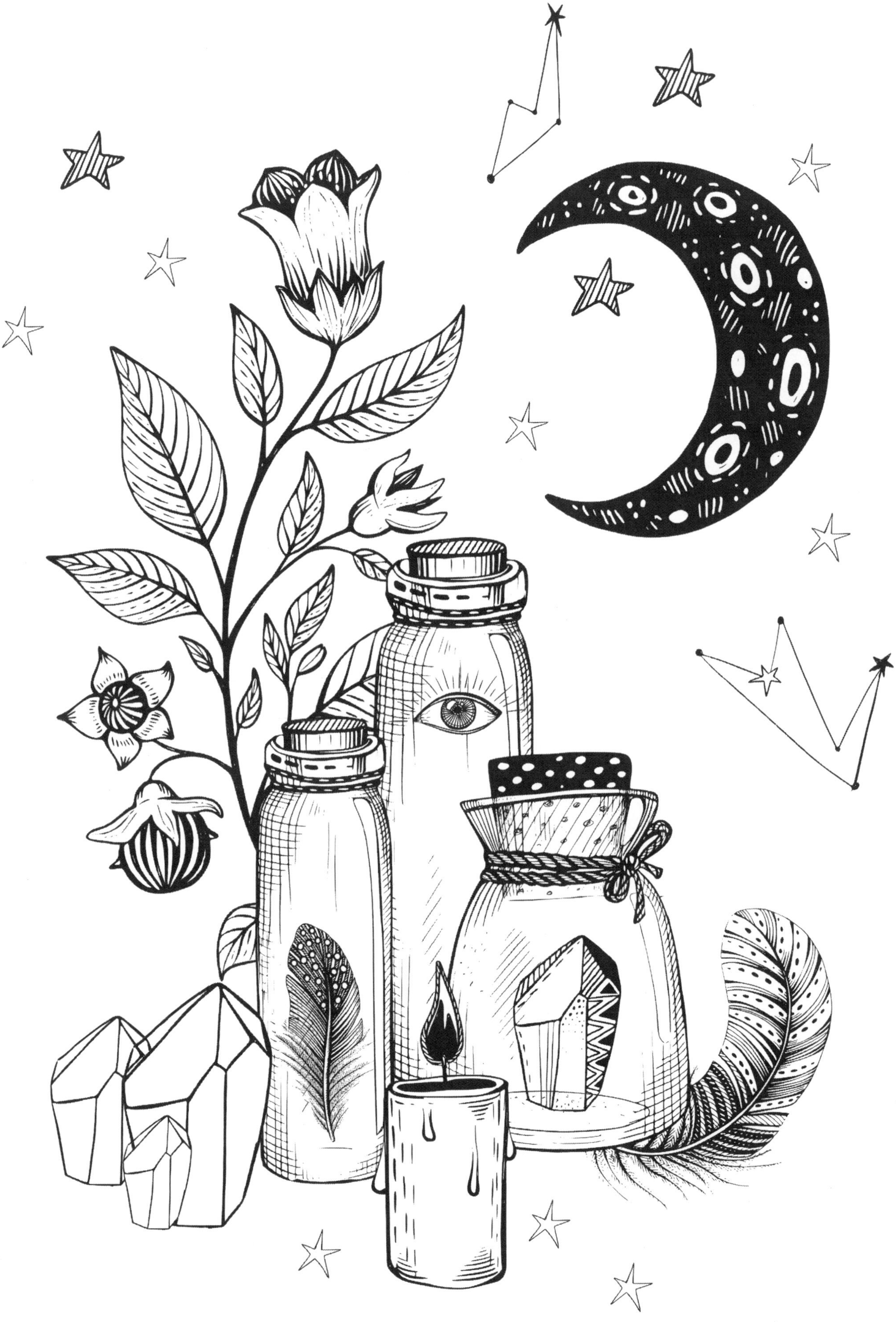

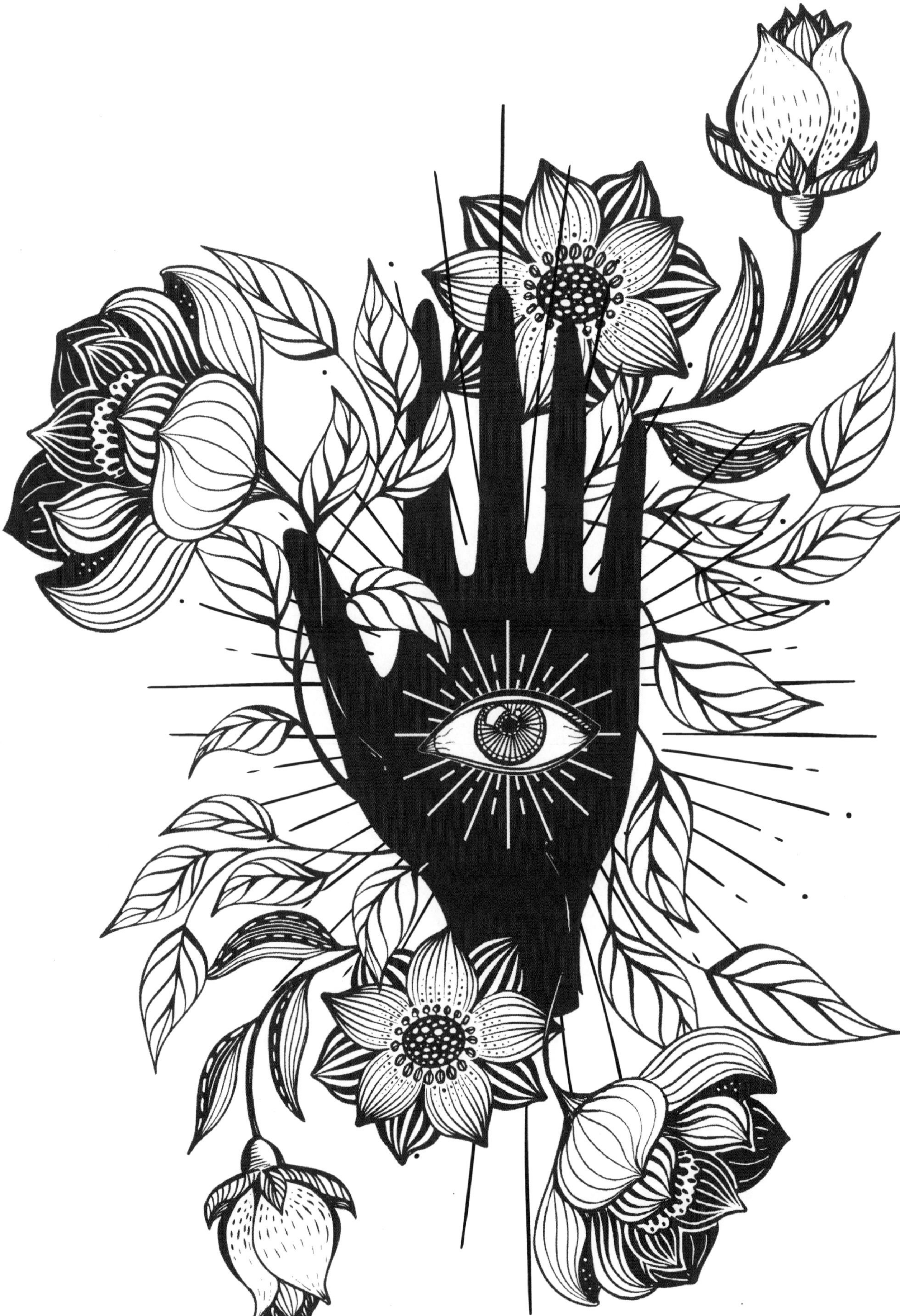

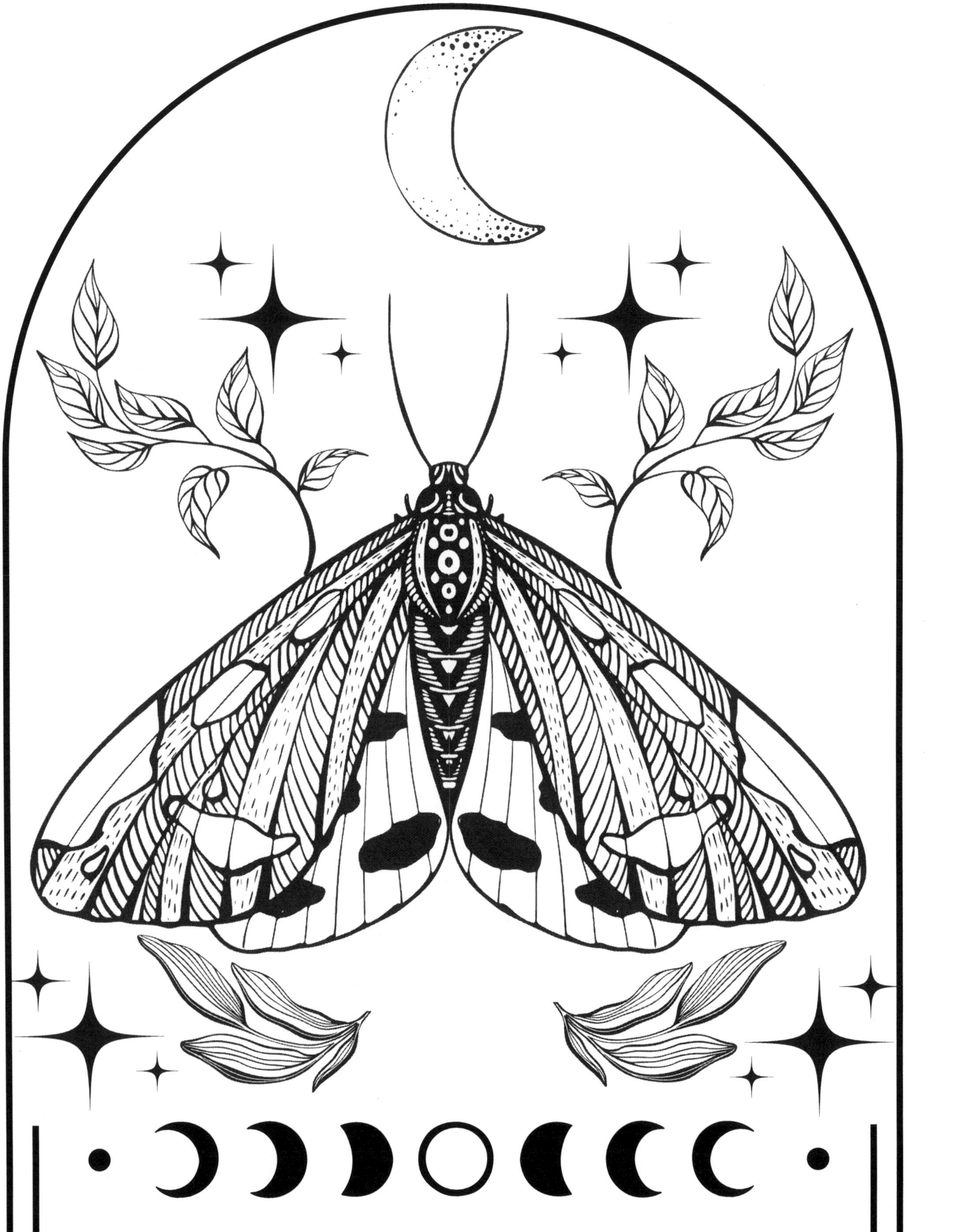

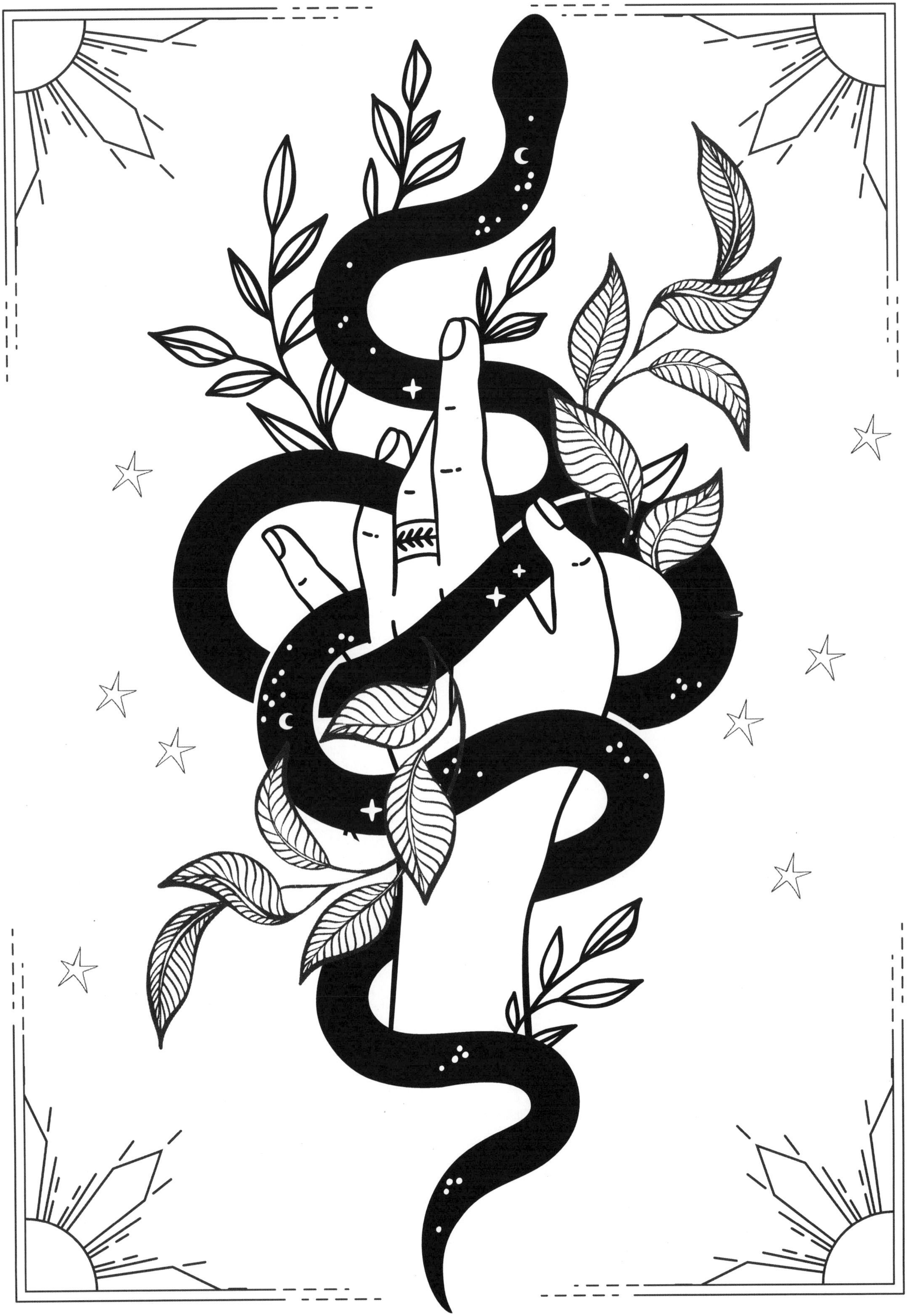

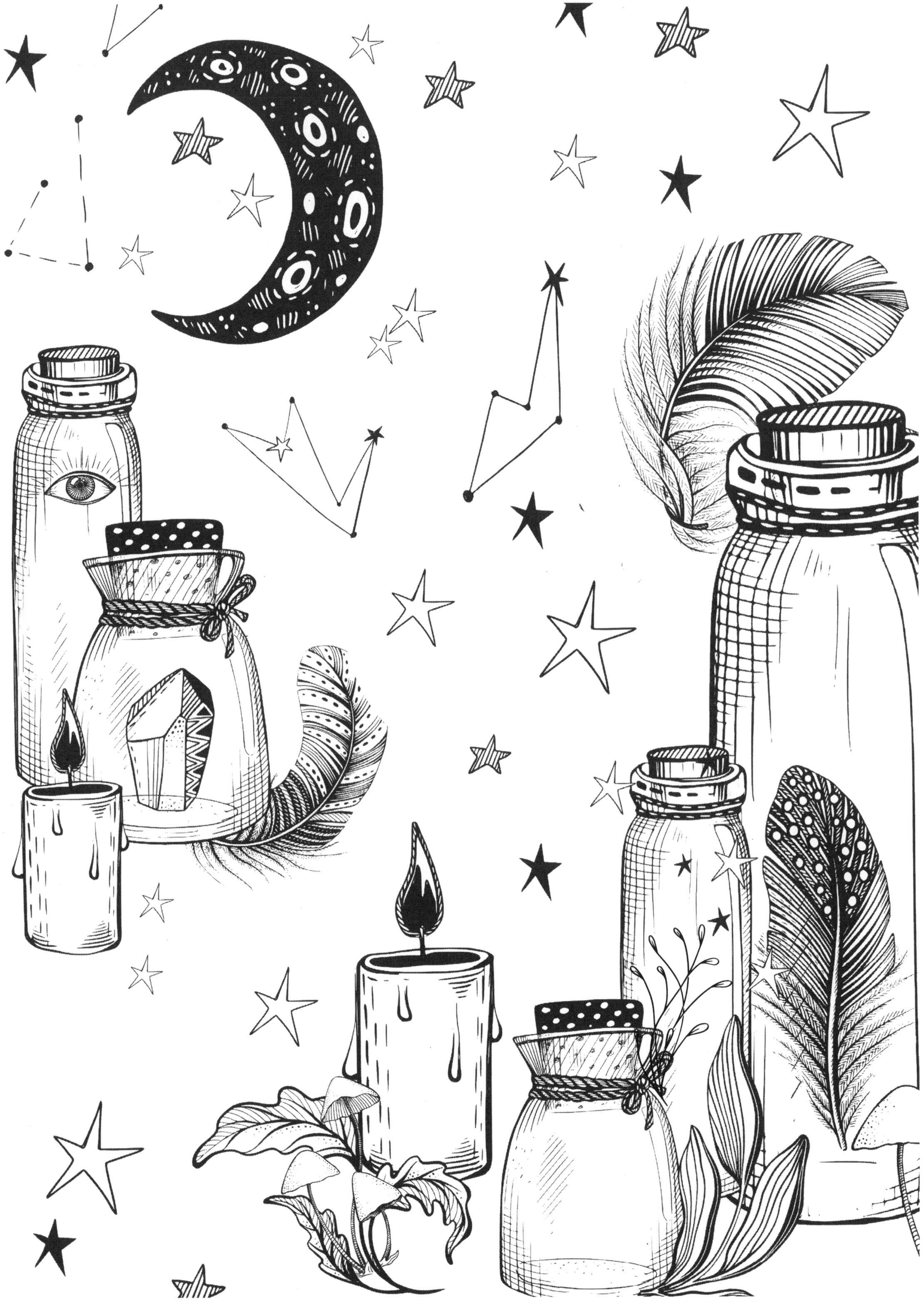

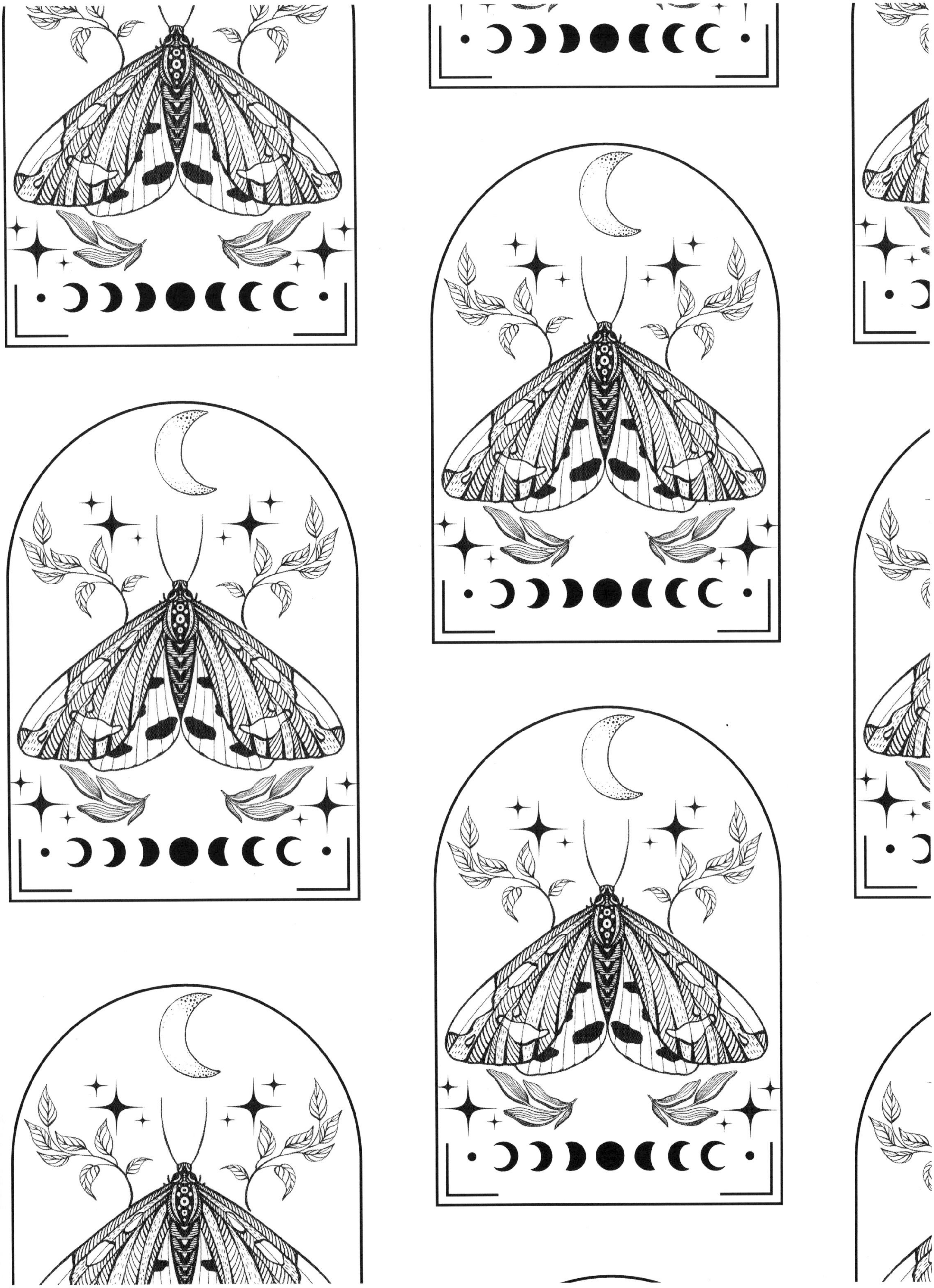

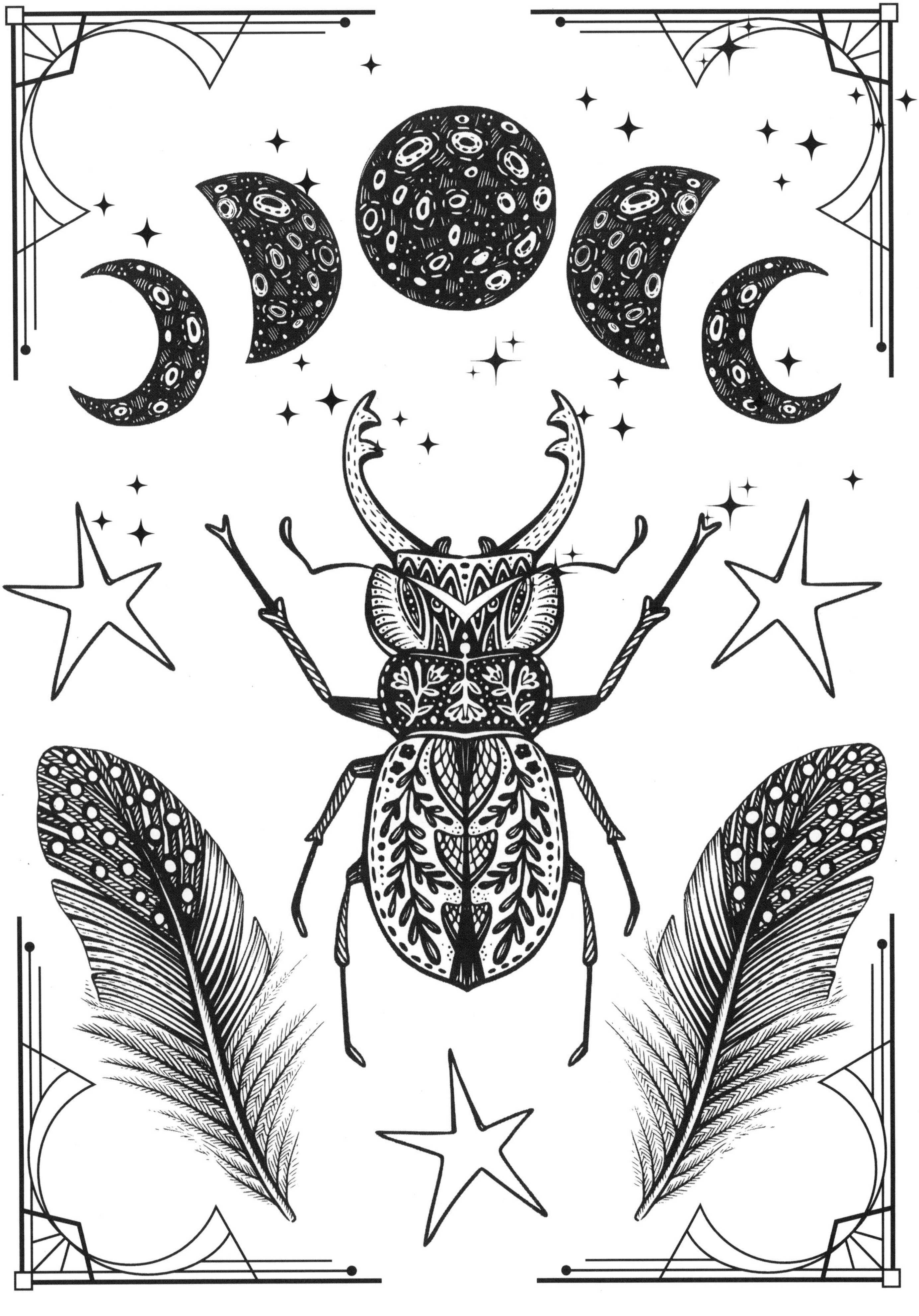

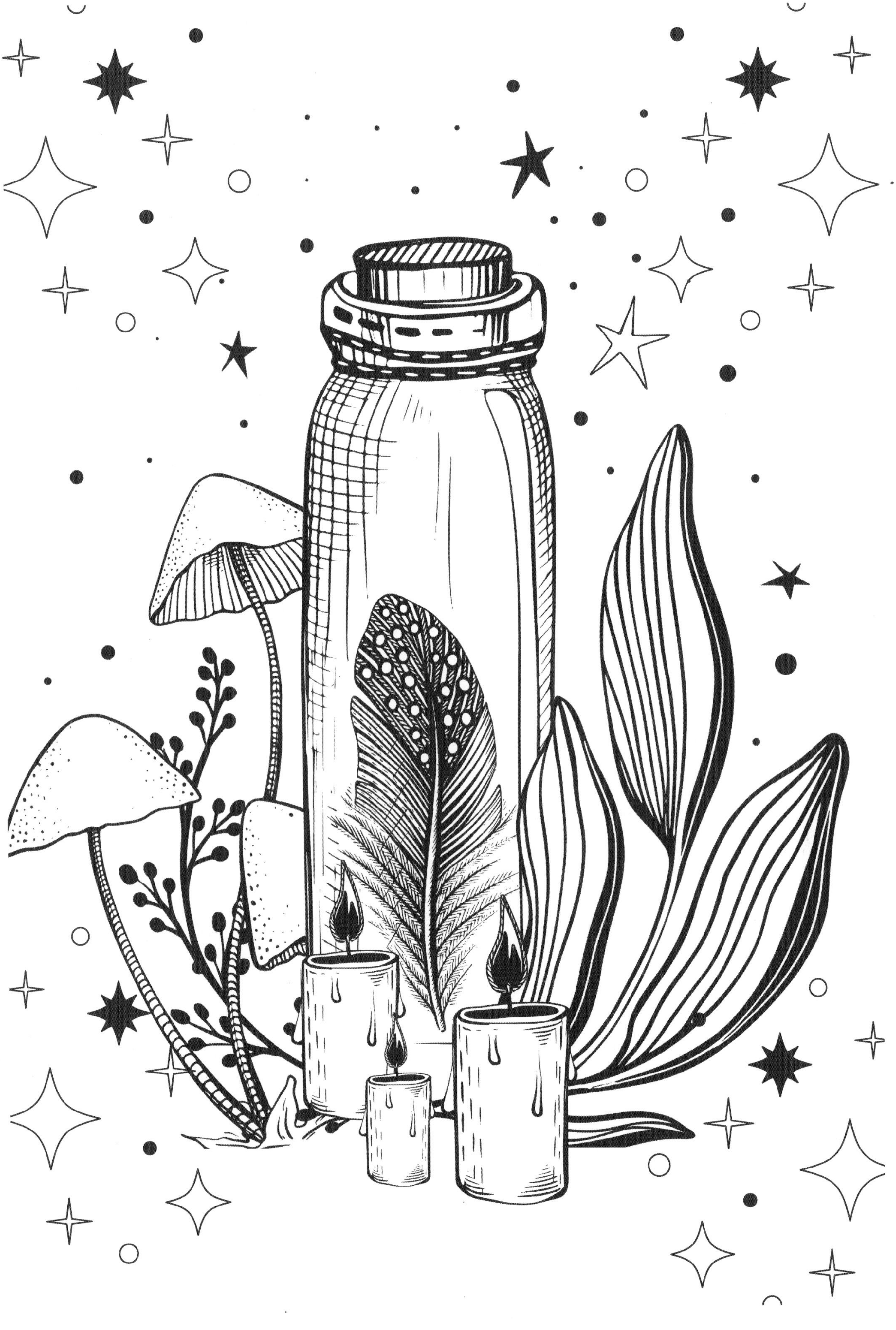

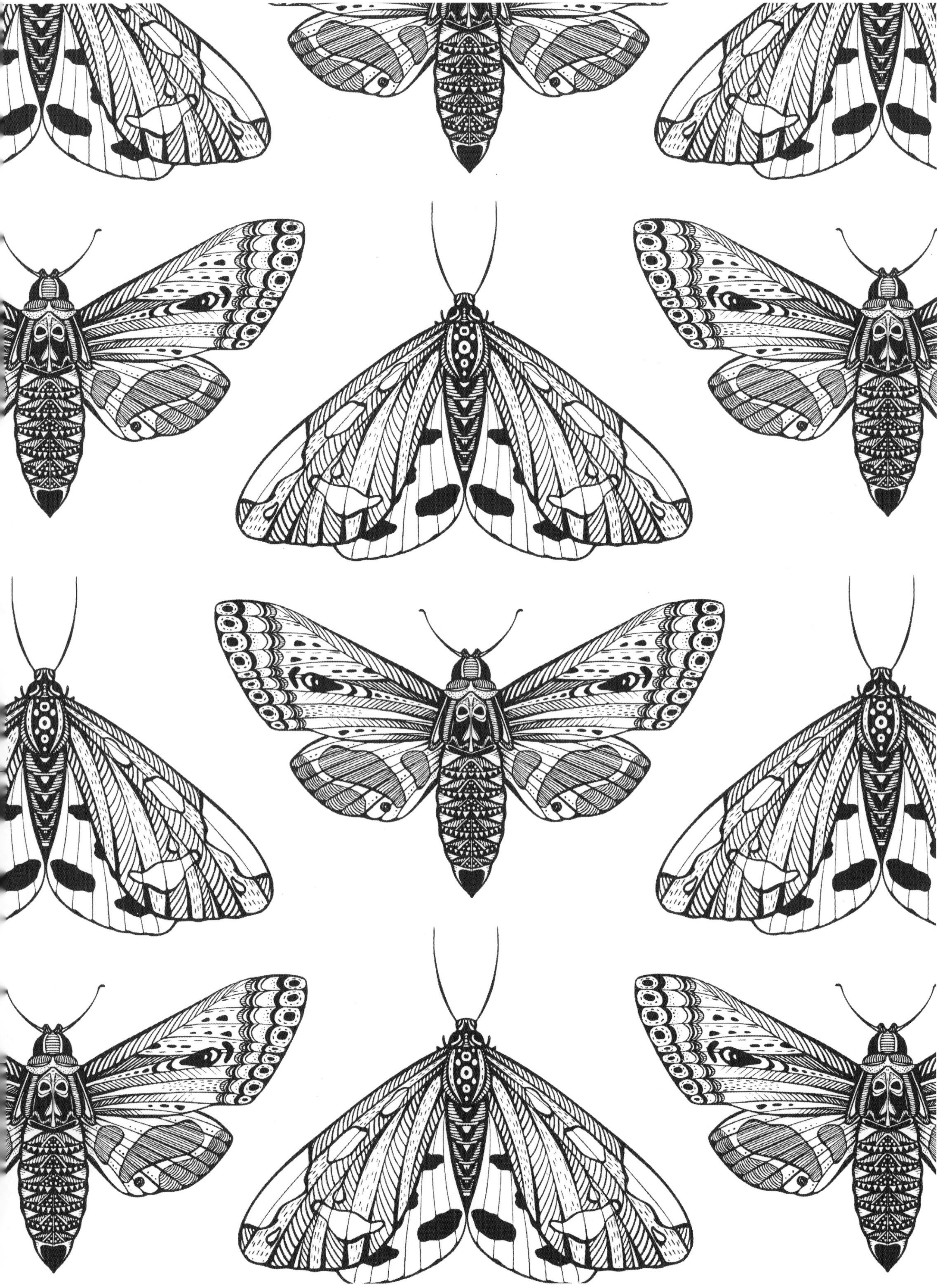

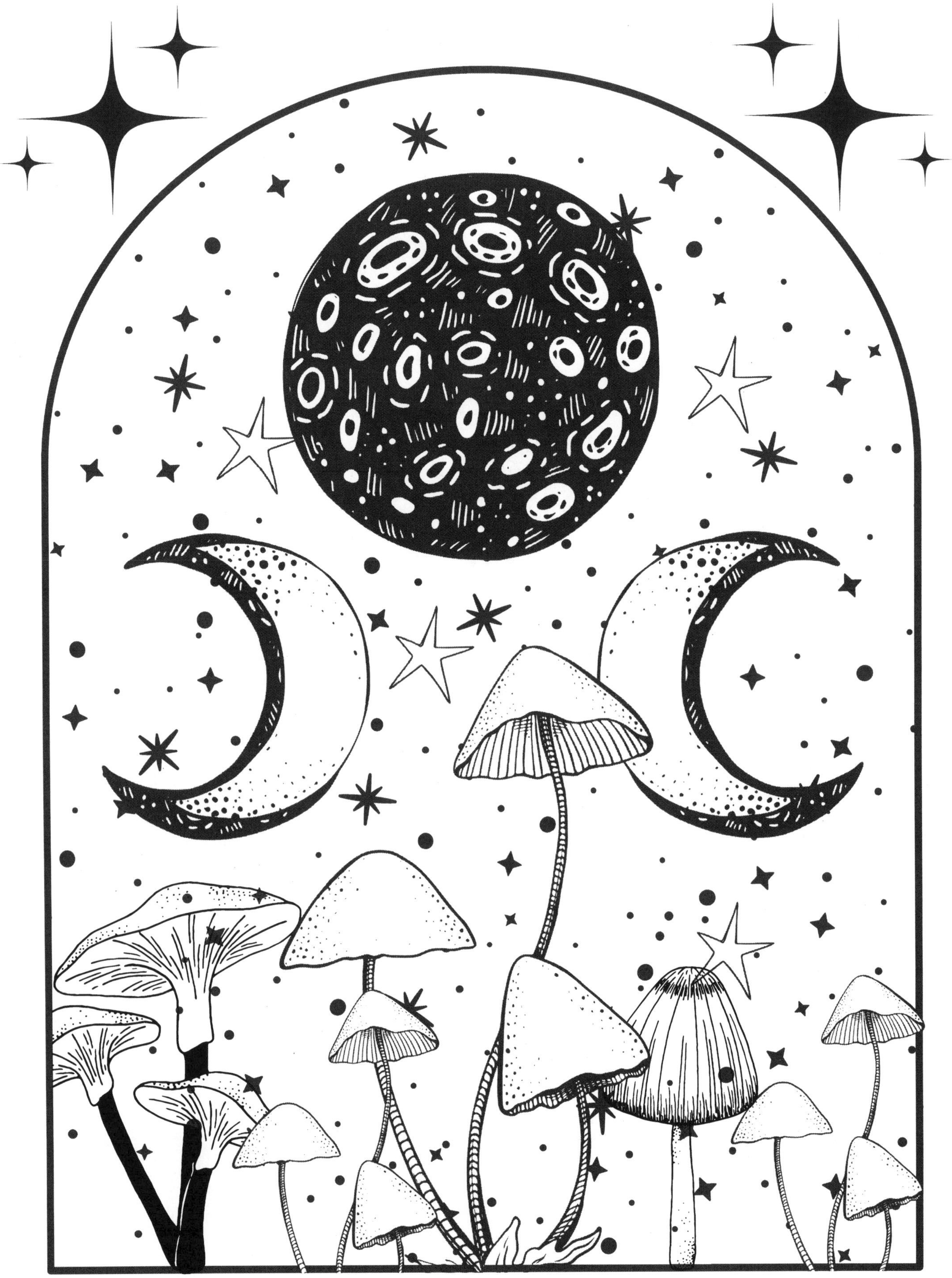

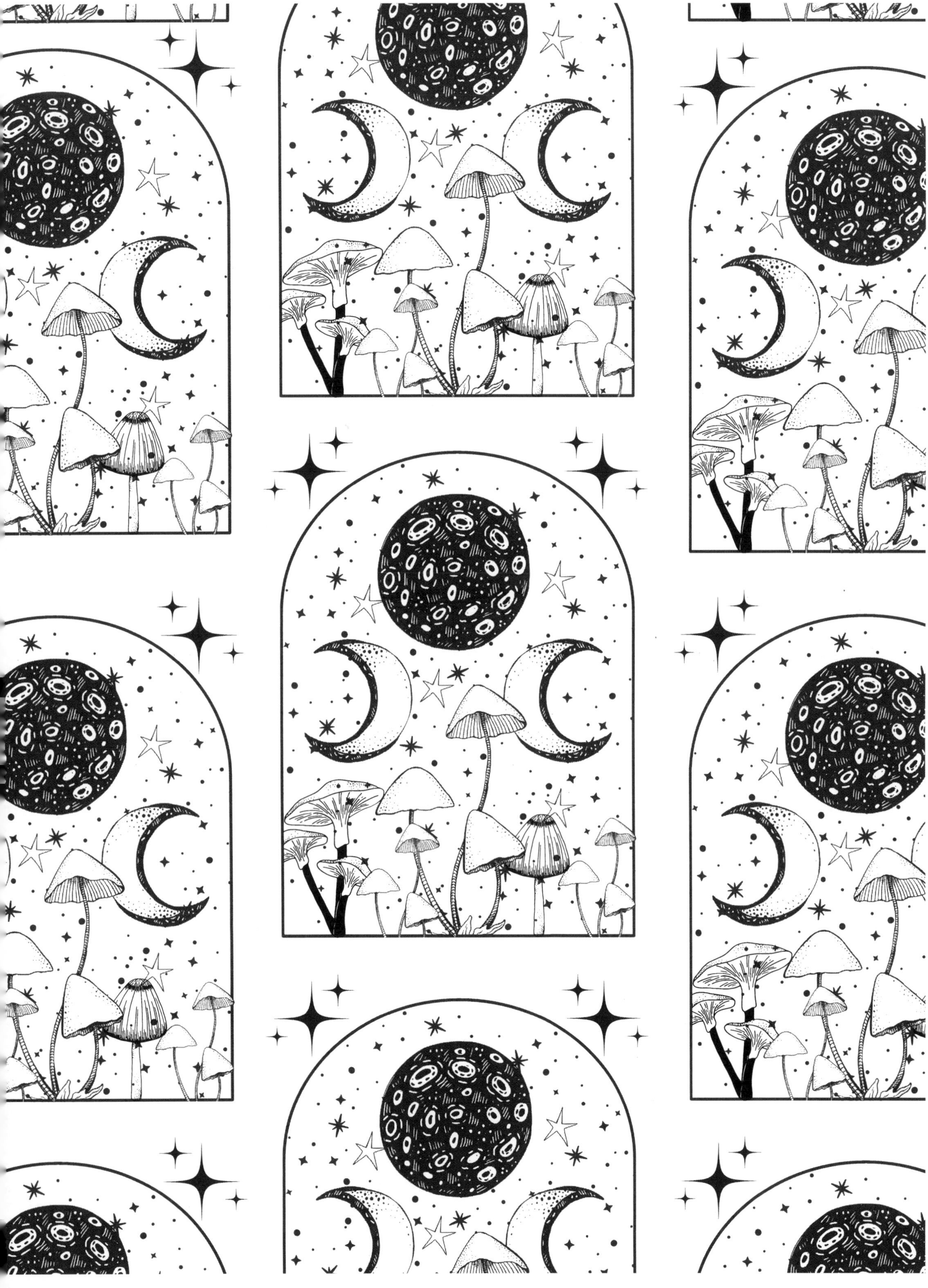

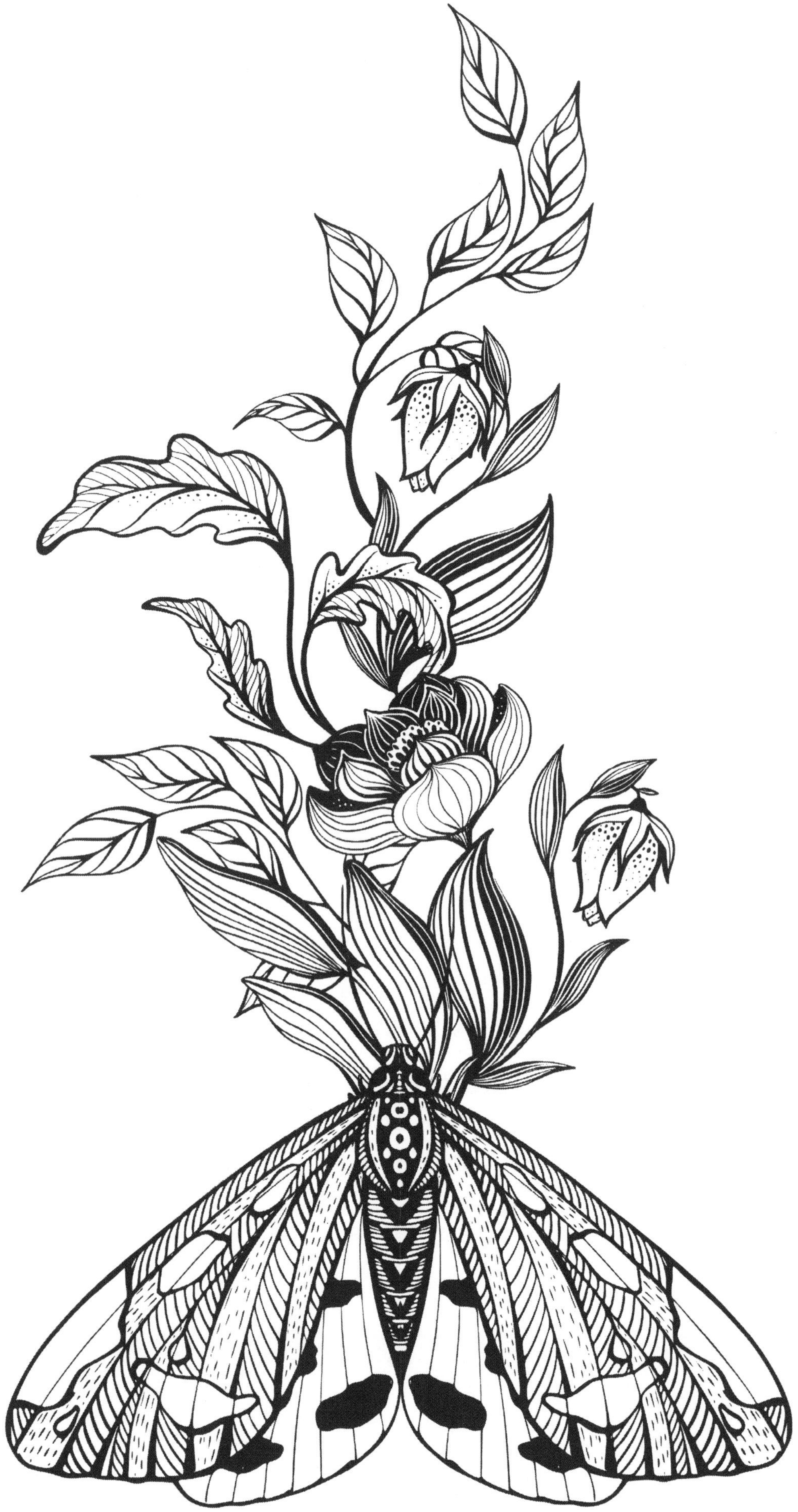

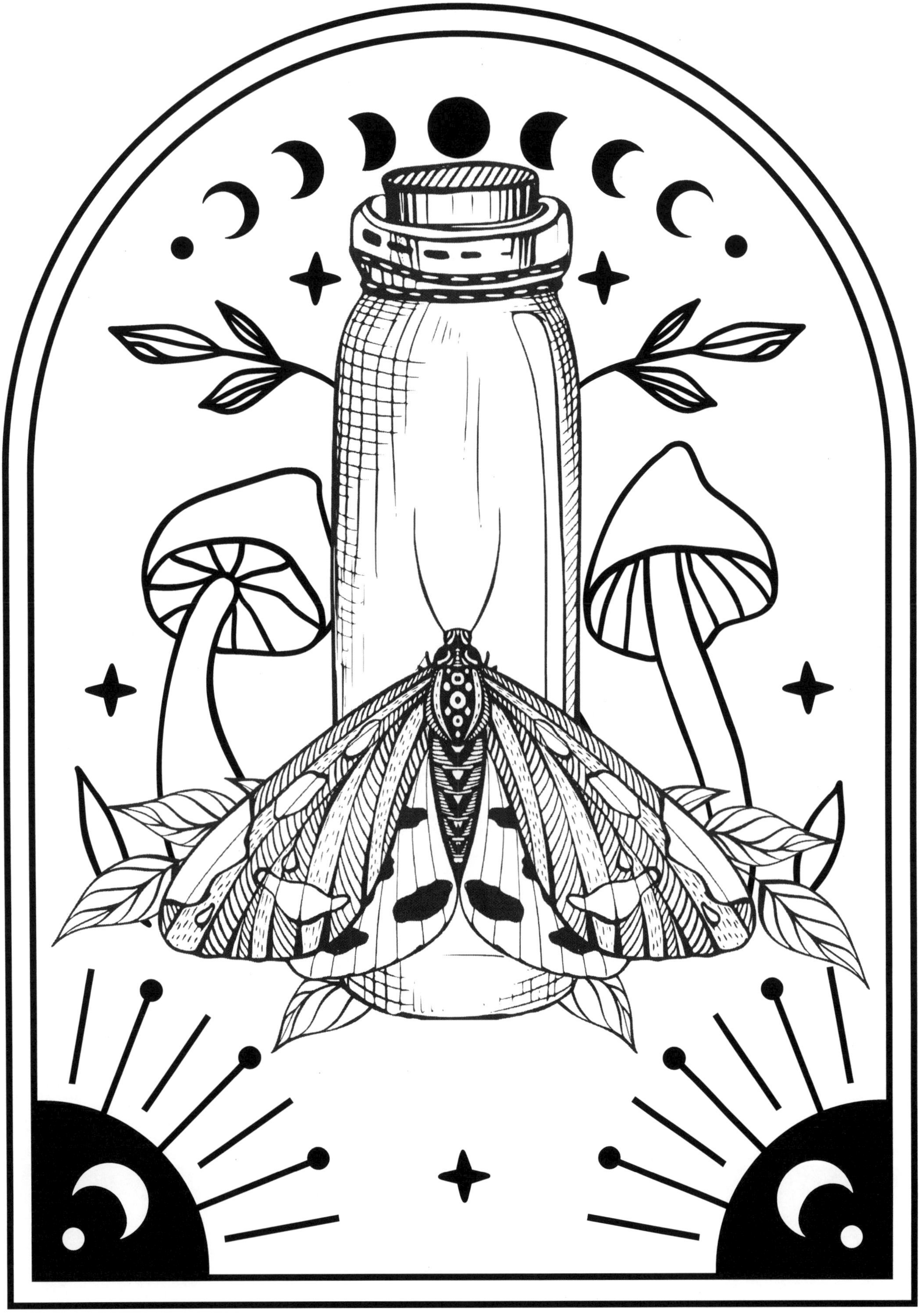

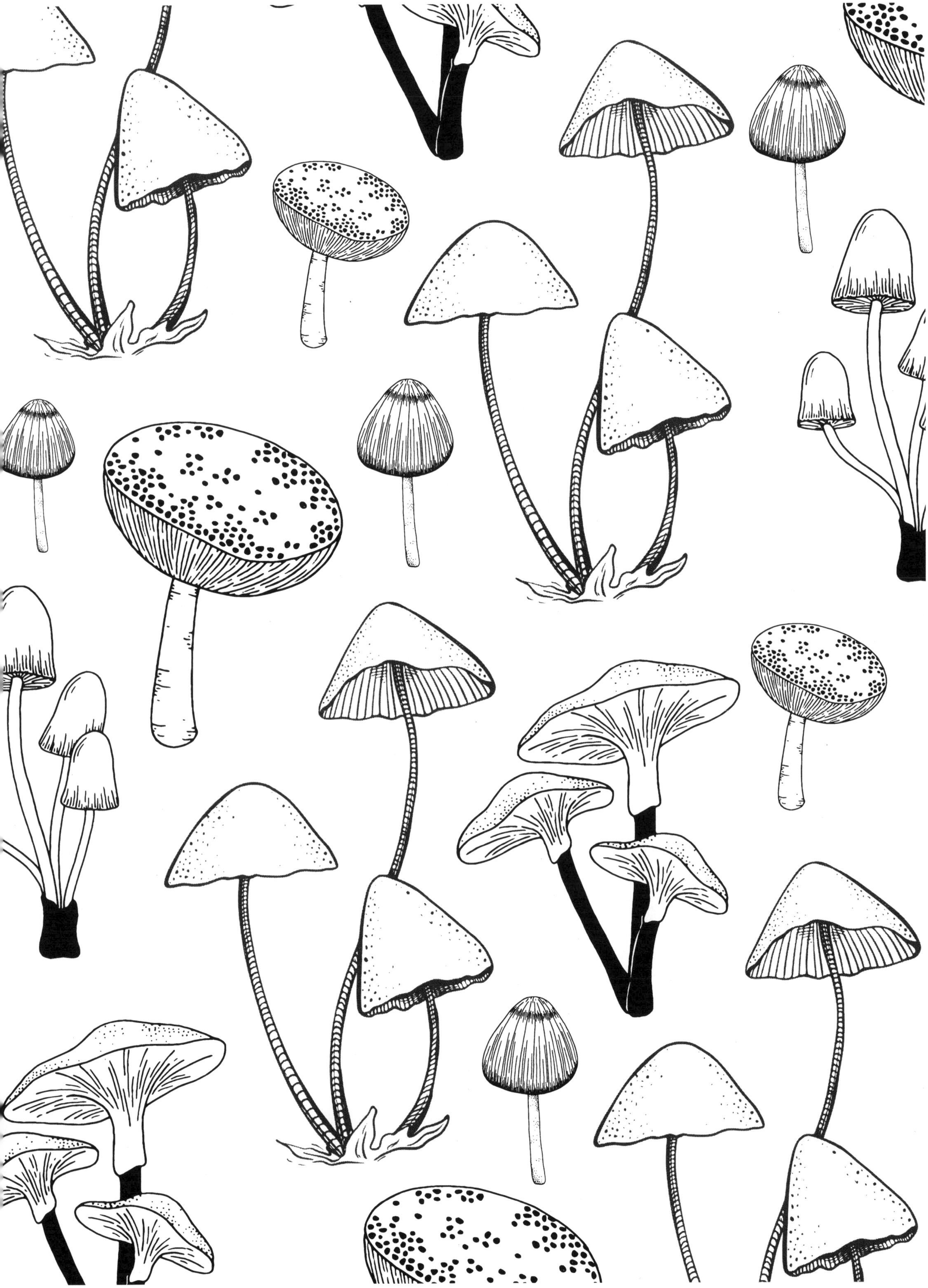

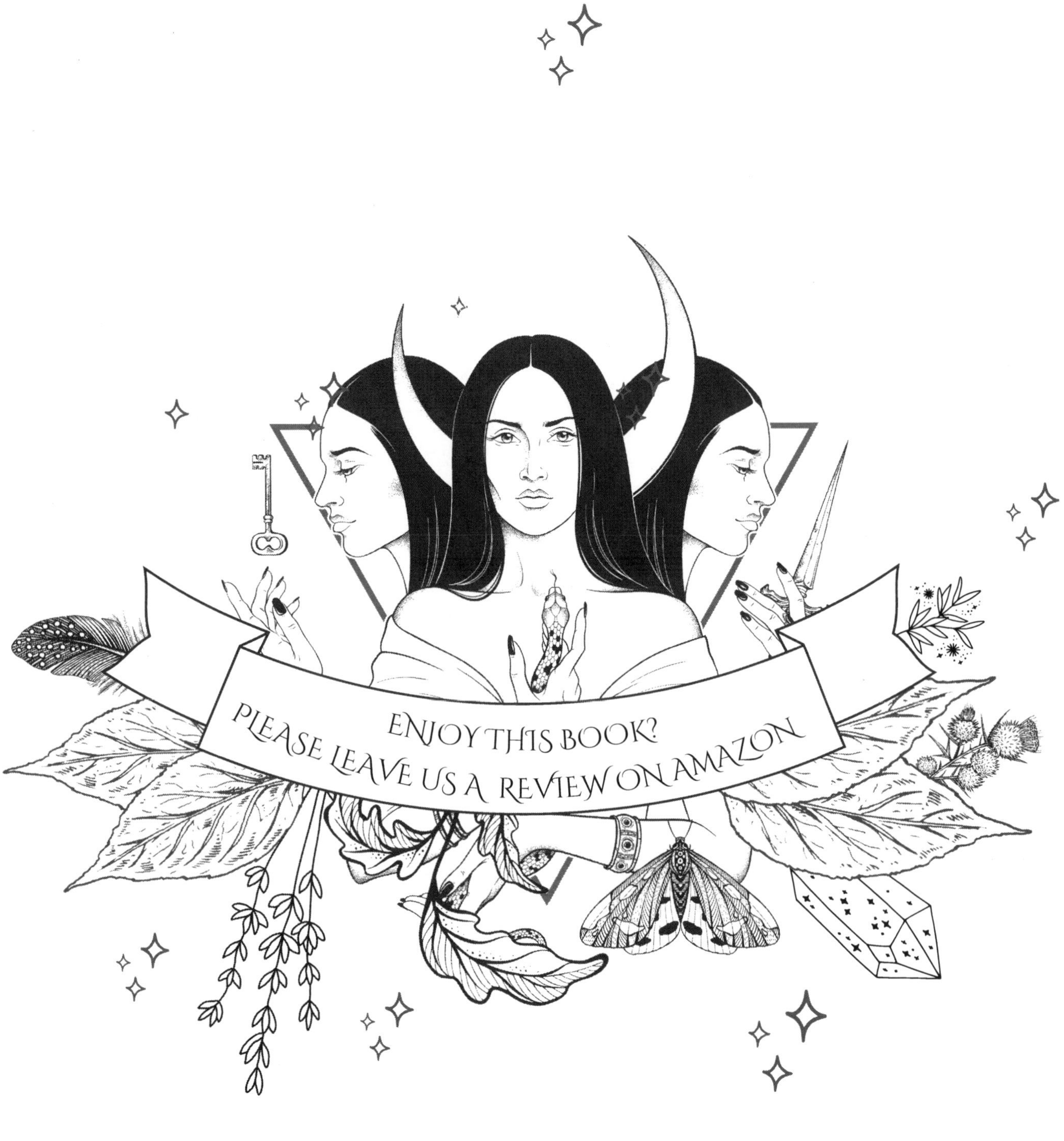
ENJOY THIS BOOK?
PLEASE LEAVE US A REVIEW ON AMAZON

Printed in Great Britain
by Amazon

16324545R00041